William Dummer Northend

**Speeches and Essays upon Political Subjects**

1860 - 1869

William Dummer Northend

**Speeches and Essays upon Political Subjects**
*1860 - 1869*

ISBN/EAN: 9783744664509

Printed in Europe, USA, Canada, Australia, Japan

Cover: Foto ©ninafisch / pixelio.de

More available books at **www.hansebooks.com**

# SPEECHES AND ESSAYS

UPON

## POLITICAL SUBJECTS,

FROM

1860 TO 1869.

BY WILLIAM D. NORTHEND.

SALEM:

PUBLISHED BY H. P. IVES.

1869.

Swasey Printing Office,
235, ESSEX STREET, SALEM.

# PREFACE.

The speeches and essays on political subjects which are collected in this volume, were delivered or published during the eventful period which has elapsed since the Presidential election of 1860.

The opinions expressed were not in accordance with the popular sentiment at the time. My purpose was to vindicate, so far as I was able, the immutable principles upon which the Union as organized by the Constitution was based; and to show the importance of that Union for the welfare and happiness of the different great Communities which composed it. Although a wide departure from these principles has been made during this period, yet I have the fullest confidence that the American people will, at no distant day, return to them with a love strengthened by their experience; and that under the organism of the past, or a more effectual one which shall be suggested by the events of this period, a harmonious co-operation, based upon the reciprocity of interests of the people of the several States, will be revived and made perpetual.

With these convictions, I submit these speeches and essays to the calm judgment of my fellow-citizens of my native County of Essex, to whom I respectfully dedicate this small volume.

SALEM, AUGUST 20th, 1869.

# CONTENTS.

# THE PERSONAL LIBERTY BILL.*

Mr. PRESIDENT—The subject which it has become our duty to consider at the present time, is one involving principles and rules of action, vastly transcending in importance the practical question of the utility of the laws which it is proposed to repeal or modify.

The subject forces irresistibly upon our minds a consideration of our duties and obligations as citizens, to sustain and give vitality to the wise and beneficent system of civil government which we have inherited, under which we live, and in which are involved all our precious hopes of the future.

By our action of to-day we shall deliberately and formally express for ourselves, and so far as we represent them, for the people of Massachusetts, whether,—irrespective of what people in other sections may do, without throwing into the balance our likes and our dislikes, our convictions for this or against that provision,—we will, to the letter and in the spirit,

---

* Delivered in the Senate of Massachusetts, February 27, 1861.

2

perform all of our obligations under the Constitution of the United States; or whether,—governed by a spirit of retaliation, by hostile opinions and determinations,—we will manifest an open contempt for. and so far as we can, nullify, objectionable provisions of that great instrument.

This government was instituted by, and its healthful existence depends upon, the will of the people, and during its continuance it is more or less efficient, gathers strength or develops weakness as it is respected and obeyed on the one hand, or traduced and its requirements evaded on the other.

And as the Constitution was based upon compromises and concessions of the different States and sections, any State or section which avails itself of the benefits and compromises in its favor, without performing its entire obligations in those matters conceded to other States in this great charter of our rights, acts unfairly towards such other States, disloyally towards the Constitution, and inflicts injuries upon the government itself, which, if persisted in, must in the end prove fatal.

From the necessity of the case, arising from the complications of the sovereignties of the State and General Governments, the Constitution must deal in general terms with many subjects, leaving it to the wisdom, patriotism, and highest interest of the people of the different sections to carry out its obvious intent honestly and in good faith.

If the people of each State and section, in a spirit unfriendly to the Constitution, should determine and undertake to legislate and act without regard to the opinions and interests of the people of other States and sections, the Constitution would become practically a nullity, and the government would not be worth preserving.

And any State which undertakes to exercise such extreme powers, except in instances where self protection absolutely requires it, commits a grievous wrong on the Constitution, and the government it created.

If experience has demonstrated that provisions of the Constitution, or legal enactments under it, are so oppressive or offensive that we cannot consent to them as our fathers did, then counsel with the people for whose benefit they were made, appeal to the ballot-box, call a convention for their change; or even, if these fail, raise the standard of revolt, which is far more honorable, and, in the end, not more destructive than acknowledging the obligations with our lips, and evading and nullifying them in our practice.

I do not mean in what I say to reproach Massachusetts for her acts in the past. She does not deserve it. I fail to see anything in her history as a Commonwealth which renders her justly amenable to any charge of disloyalty. She has performed her full duty when it was repugnant to the best and highest feelings of her citizens. She has uttered her complaints and expressed her convictions when she has felt that the general government was too severe in its exactions, but she has always obeyed all its legal requirements.

And sir, I am not prepared to pass a censorious judgment upon her for the enactment of the laws of 1855, with her apprehensions of danger to her citizens from the indefensible severity of the fugitive slave law of 1850; they were passed before the fugitive slave law had been declared constitutional by the United States Court, and their precise legal effect was not sufficiently considered by the Legislature.

But when our attention is now directed toward them, and from a careful examination we have reason to believe that they are in conflict with legal enactments under the Constitution of the United States, I do say that we may for the first time put Massachusetts clearly and culpably in the wrong, by refusing to repeal them, or to so modify them as to relieve them of all objections of unconstitutionality.

And to a full understanding of our obligations under the acts of Congress relating to the rendition of fugitive slaves, it will be useful to refer to the circumstances connected with, and reasons for, the provision in the Constitution of the United States upon the subject. It is obvious to every one that

the Constitution could not have been adopted and
the Union consummated, unless the North had con-
sented that slavery remain in the States where it
existed, and with that acknowledged fact it became
necessary, as an incident to it, that the owners should
have the right to retake their slaves if they escaped
into other States in the Confederacy; without this,
slavery could hardly exist in the Border States, and
a powerful temptation would be offered to those opposed to the system in the Free States to aid
in the escape of fugitives, and thus a serious
source of difficulty in the future would be opened.
Accordingly a provision was inserted in the Constitution that "no person held to service or labor in
one State, under the laws thereof, escaping into another, shall in consequence of any law or regulation
therein be discharged from such service or labor,
but shall be delivered up on claim of the party to
whom such service or labor may be due." This
was adopted by the convention unanimously; and
in the convention of this State, called for its ratification, composed of our ablest and best men, no objection was made to this provision. And this was
not the first instance of the recognition of such a
law. In the ordinance of 1787, drawn up by Na-
than Dane, was a similar provision. And in the
earlier history of our country we find the same necessity acknowledged.

In 1643 the Colonies of Massachusetts Bay, Ply-

mouth, Connecticut and New Haven entered into articles of Confederacy, in which was the following stipulation : "It is also agreed, if any servant run away
from his master into any other of these confederated
jurisdictions, that in such cases, upon the certificate of
one magistrate in the jurisdiction out of which the
said servant fled, or upon other due proof, the said
servant shall be delivered either to his master or
any other that pursues and brings such certificate of
proof." And in 1650 a compact was made between
this Confederacy and New Netherlands, in which it
was agreed that "the same way and course" concerning fugitives should be adopted.

Thus it will be seen that the provision in the
Constitution concerning fugitive slaves was in conformity to precedent, and was a necessary consequence of the compromises of that instrument.
And in accordance with the Constitution it was
legitimate for Congress to legislate for the purpose
of carrying into effect this provision, and accordingly, in 1793, Congress enacted a law for the rendition of slaves. This passed the senate without
division, and there were only seven votes against it
in the house, of which one was from Massachusetts,
one from Virginia, and one from Maryland. This
law remained in force for half a century without
any serious objection. In 1842, a slave (Latimer)
was incarcerated in one of our jails under circumstances of aggravation, and the same year the

Supreme Court of the United States, in the case of Prigg *vs.* Commonwealth of Pennsylvania, held that the States were not obliged to aid in the execution of the law, which induced and justified the law enacted by the next session of our legislature, which prohibited the use of our jails for the purposes of the fugitive slave law, and forbade certain State magistrates from taking part in cases of rendition.

In 1850, a supplementary fugitive slave law was passed by Congress, containing many odious and harsh provisions.

The people of the free States believed that the very severity of the law would prevent its successful operation, and waited in the hope that it would be declared void by the judicial tribunals.

In 1854, a slave (Burns) was returned into slavery from Boston, under circumstances which created much excitement in the Commonwealth, and the legislature, in 1855, enacted laws which, with the laws of 1843, constitute the so-called *"Personal Liberty Bill."*

The attention of the legislature of 1856 was directed to the anomalous provisions of this law, and a bill for its repeal passed the house of representatives, when intelligence of an assault upon one of our senators in Congress prevented its further passage; and it is very clear that had it not been for this outrage, this law would have been swept from the statute books by that, the first republican legislature of this State.

In 1858 the attention of the legislature was directed to the law, and upon the recommendation of governor Banks, some of the most objectionable portions of it were repealed. For reasons stated in his recent message, he did not advise further revision of it at that time, although in his judgment it was proper that further revision should be made.

Our attention is now directed to it by the use that has been made of it as a pretext in other States, and also by petitions from a large and respectable portion of our own citizens; and a large committee of both branches have patiently and fully considered the entire subject, and made a unanimous report as the result of their deliberations, which we are now called upon to consider.

In my judgment the bill proposed by the Committee relieves the law from unconstitutional objections, and should be passed as reported, although with my convictions of the slight practical value of the law, and of the sufficient protection our laws afford without it. I should have preferred an unconditional repeal of all, excepting the section relating to kidnapping.

The original personal liberty act, in the recent revision of our statutes, was divided up, and in our general statutes is to be found in the 144th chapter, under the titles of personal liberty, and *habeas corpus*, and I would call your attention briefly to a consideration of the different sections. Under the head of personal liberty, sections 58 and 59 provide for the defence of alleged fugitives at the expense of the State. Sections 60 and 67 forbid persons holding certain offices under the State from aiding in cases of rendition, and certain United States officers from holding certain State offices. We may legally enact such prohibitions, although of little practical value to the alleged fugitive; the objection to them, if any exists, is in the penalties attached to them.

Sections 63, 64 and 65 forbid sheriffs, militia, &c., from rendering any aid in cases of rendition. It·is contended, and fairly I think, that these sections forbid the employment of the militia to suppress any popular outbreak in cases of rendition. This is wrong and in bad faith. It manifests a disposition to nullify the law by giving license to a mob to obstruct its exercise and violate the peace without any resistance from the authorities. This objection is met and relieved by the bill of the Committee. Section 62 provides for punishing the offence of kidnapping. This is clearly a proper subject for legislation, but as under this section a liability attaches to a person acting honestly under a supposed right, the Committee have reported an amendment which relieves it of this objection. The above are all of the sections under the head of "Personal Liberty," intended to have any effect in cases of rendition.

3

I now propose to consider the sections of the *habeas corpus* law relating to this subject. They are the 6th, 19th, 20th and 21st sections of said 144th chapter.

They are intended to authorize—

1st.  The taking of the fugitive from restraint.

2d.  A trial by jury upon all matters in the return of the officer, "*or alleged.*"

3d.  Pleadings and rules of evidence on the trial, of an anomalous character.

So far as these sections are intended for the purpose of authorizing the taking of the alleged fugitive from the custody of the United States Marshals, by an officer of this Commonwealth, or for a trial by jury upon the question whether service or labor is due, or to hinder and obstruct the execution of the law by unusual and anomalous proceedings on the trial, they conflict with laws of the United States; as the Constitution provides that "The Constitution, and the laws of the United States which shall be made in pursuance thereof,  *  *  * shall be the supreme law of the land; and the judges of every State shall be bound thereby, anything in the Constitution or laws of any State to the contrary notwithstanding."

Section 6 provides for the form of the writ of *habeas corpus*, to be directed to the sheriff and his deputies, in cases of restraint by persons not sheriffs, deputy sheriffs, coroners or jailors.  By the Re-

vised Statutes, cases of restraint by the marshal
and his deputies were included.    These have
been striken out since.  From a literal construction of
this section, which is aided by our previous legislation just stated, it is clearly the intent that our
sheriff shall be authorized to take from the custody
—from the hands—of the United States Marshal,
the alleged fugitive, whom he may have under a
proper warrant under the authority of the United
States laws; and if that is the construction of it,
there is no one who doubts that the provision is
unconstitutional.  We have no right, we can have no
power, by any State law, to take a man out of the
custody of the United States Marshal, held under a
proper warrant.  If, in any way, the Marshal can,
by summons or otherwise, be brought before a State
tribunal; if he there shows that he holds the prison-
er by a warrant under the laws of the United States,
issued by a court of competent jurisdiction, then
our courts can go not one step further.  They have
no right to inquire into the constitutionality of the
law under which that warrant was issued; they
have no right to go back of that warrant and inquire into the question whether service was due
from the fugitive, which was the basis of the proceeding upon which that warrant was issued.  They
can only look at the papers; they can only pass
upon the question whether the person holding him
is a United States officer, and whether the process

was issued by a proper officer or court, under the authority of the United States; and back of that there is no authority, and there can be no power, in any of our State courts, to act. If this law goes further,—if it is intended to permit a fugitive slave a trial, by jury or by the court, upon the question whether he owes service or labor,—that would be clearly unconstitutional. There is no jury, and no court, that can have the power, in this State, to pass upon the question whether a slave, properly in the hands of the Marshal, owes service or labor. The statute is to this effect: that the alleged fugitive shall have a trial by jury, and that upon that trial the jury shall pass upon those particular matters contained in the return of the officer, or alleged. This being a civil proceeding, any matters may be alleged on either side, and it may be alleged that he was not a fugitive, or did not owe service; and the jury, under this law, are empowered, and it is their duty, to pass upon the subject, and bring in a general verdict, which shall be final and conclusive. I submit that if this is the construction of the law, it is clearly and unqualifiedly in contravention of the laws of the United States.

Then in regard to the evidence. It seems to me that when we undertake to depart from the usual modes of trial, and institute a new and anomalous mode, one which puts burdens which are unprecedented upon the party claiming· in the court, and when that is made to apply to a law of the United States upon this subject, and to no other, it is certainly offensive to that government, it is certainly open to the objection that it is an attempt, upon our part, to interfere with and delay proceedings under a law of the United States.

The bill proposed by the Committee entirely relieves this law of these objections.

The bill of the Committee proceeds further to provide that the sheriff, after he has served the writ, may make his return thereof only to the Justices of the Supreme Court, instead of to the Justices of the Supreme Court and of the Superior Court, as provided by the present law. That point has been properly commented upon by the Chairman, [Mr. Stone,] and every one who is cognizant of the proceedings in court, knows that this is for the protection and for the benefit of any one who seeks redress under a writ of *habeas corpus.* I am willing and desirous, in this matter. to give all the aid and protection which it is within the power of the legislature to give, and I do not wish to take away any legal immunities the fugitive may properly have under our laws.

This is the last provision. The bill of the Committee, in my opinion, provides for the relief of the constitutional objections to the law as it now stands.

There are few in the community who do not believe

that the law in regard to personal liberty and
*habeas corpus* should be construed as this Committee
have construed it.   I do not think that there is any
one who, with a view to our obligations under the
Constitution of the United States, will not admit
that the law should be thus construed.    There are
some who believe that with this construction the act
is valid.   But I do not see how any one one can hold
that opinion in regard to these two sections, without very grave doubt, in opposition to the opinion of some of our ablest and most learned jurists.

Many will feel regret that the law, with this construction, will be of little practical value. For,
if a fugitive slave is arrested by the United States
Marshal or his deputy, under a warrant, and there
is no power to take him out of their hands, the
law can be of no benefit to fugitives in that
class of cases.    It is the largest class, and with
this construction would, of course, be the only class
in the future.   For no person who should come to
Massachusetts to retake his slave would come and
undertake to do it personally, when he could be protected by a warrant, and act under the authority of
a United States Commissioner.   For this reason I
consider the law of little practical value to the
fugitive.   It may still be of possible benefit to
him if he should be arrested by his owner without
a warrant.   And if, as is contended, the law as it
will remain, or as it should properly be construed,

operates to give to the slave an opportunity to
raise questions of law to further test any provisions
of the fugitive slave law, then certainly I should desire that he should have the benefit of it.  And if I
believed that privilege was one material to him in any
respect, I should certainly not entertain the views I
now hold in regard to the repeal of the entire act.

But, sir, there are many who have doubted the
propriety of making any revision of these laws,
from an apprehension that if they were repealed, no
safeguard would be left for our personal liberties.
We are told that any individual might with impunity be dragged from his house, in the night time—
that there is nothing to protect the free citizens of
Massachusetts, if these laws are repealed, or of no
effect.  Why, sir, if these laws are repealed, we
have still remaining upon our statute-books the provisions of the law of *habeas corpus* which have protected our people in the past, and which are capable of protecting them amply in the future.  We
have the most admirable system of *habeas corpus*.
Any person who may be improperly in restraint may
demand the writ, precisely the same as under this
law, even if constitutional.  In the first proceeding,
—in the proceeding of rescuing a man from immediate danger, there is not a pretended provision in the
personal liberty act which gives him any protection
over the *habeas corpus* laws, which would remain if
the whole act of 1855 were repealed.  The writ of

*habeas corpus* would be *issued* as now by any Judge
of the Supreme, Superior, Probate or Police Courts,
and if none known to be within five miles, then by
any Justice of the Peace. That, after all, is the
great point of importance to the community;
because, there is no one who can reasonably
doubt but that if a person improperly restrained
is taken out of the hands of those who im-
prison him, by a writ of this Commonwealth,
and brought before the Supreme Judicial Court, his
rights will be secured to him, whether it be by the
wisdom of the Court, or by a trial by jury, with the
protections afforded by this bill.

Mr. President, we have ample securities for every
one, for the white man, for the black man, for· the
freeman and for the fugitive. It is, sir, the great
objection to this act,—that our laws had already
covered the whole ground, and that we have full protection without going beyond them and infringing
upon the Constitution and laws of the United States.

But it is further objected to the repeal or modification of these laws, that although the arguments
against them which I have suggested may be well
founded,—although there may be doubt with regard
to their constitutionality, yet we should let them
remain until the Court has declared them void. To
such I would say that it is of importance, always,
that all laws be clear, and particularly that a law of
this character, which affects rights of persons in

other States, should not be misunderstood. It is important further that the law should not hold out a false security to those who are intended to be benefitted by its provisions. We do injustice to the fugitive, if we hold out to him an apparent protection when he has none in fact. It is right for him, for us, and for the people of other States, that there should be no ground for misconstruction of our laws upon this subject.

Another objection urged is, that it is not now the time to take this action,—that the existence of these laws upon our Statute Book has been used by dishonest men in other States to our discredit and to the disadvantage of the country. There is no doubt, Mr. President, that this is true. But the men who have used such arguments have used them as *pretexts*— they have used them to overpower Union men in the Southern States—in South Carolina, in Georgia, and in other seceding States, with more or less effect. I would do nothing at this time with the expectation of influencing the people of those States, as they are situated. . But there is another class of people—there is another class of States, upon which, if this modification can have any beneficial effect, it seems to me all will desire it. There are the Border States, so called—there are the States of Virginia, of Kentucky, Missouri, Tennessee, Delaware, Maryland—States which, with all the efforts that have been made to seduce them, with all the excite-

4

ments in the Gulf States, have as yet remained true and loyal to the Union. And it is not without difficulty that it has been so. The Union men in those States have had to contend against great odds. They have had to fight against this spirit which has come in upon them from the neighboring States, and some of them have thus far achieved glorious results. If, by any action, we can strengthen the hands and cheer the hearts of these noble men who are fighting for the Constitution and the Union, should we not do it? I think there is no one who would not rejoice, if in any way he could aid them in their patriotic struggles.

It is of the greatest importance, in my judgment to the future of this people, that these States remain true. Sir, notwithstanding all that has happened, I have a faith that we shall live to see the day when every State which has ever been connected with the Union will be in the Union. I have a belief that when the hour of madness has passed away, one by one, these States will return, to remain, without compulsion—without coercion. And until that time, these noble border States will stand as they have stood, with us. Their people will have met the reproaches of the people of the slave States of the South. They will have taken us by the hand; we shall have talked with them as we have never talked with people of the slave States before, and they will have talked with us as they

never talked with us before; we shall have opened
our hearts to them and they theirs to us; we shall
have removed all the doubts and misunderstandings
that existed between us, and they will see us as we
are, true and patriotic men, as they have not before
believed us to be. If these States remain in the
Union, it never stood so strong as it will stand
under these circumstances. These Border States,
situate between us and the States of the Gulf, will be
the conservative States; and if the States of the
Gulf shall return, there can be no pretext used from
which the people of the Border States will not defend the North, nothing in which they will not stand
by the North. Let us do all we can, honorably and
properly, that may aid the people of the Border
States to understand our real sentiments, and that
will give strength and courage to their Union loving
men.

Sir, I feel a solicitude that in this crisis of our
national affairs Massachusetts should stand above
reproach or even suspicion. I will not consider, for
it is not the time nor the occasion, whether other
States have done their duty. We all have our convictions upon this point. We are only now to consider whether Massachusetts shall do her duty.
If we can go before the country with no stain of
disloyalty on our garments, with a consciousness
that no enactment of our beloved Commonwealth
affords just cause of offence to our brethren in other

States, we carry with us an immense moral influence; we present an example which in the present, and more in the future, will have a commanding influence upon our sister States. Sir, the ways of Providence in their inception and progress are often mysterious to us, but it is not unfrequently given to man to trace back their unerring courses from the final results. And, sir, I have felt oftentimes that as a people we have not any of us appreciated our blessings as we should—that in the enjoyment of unequalled privileges for nearly a century under the wonderful system which our fathers inaugurated, we have forgotten that their continuance depends upon the performance by us of some disagreeable duties. And, sir, if the present unhappy state of the country shall lead us all, in all the States, back to the living fountains from which our fathers drank—if it will cause us to forget our animosities and estrangements, and bring us all, North and South, East and West, with fraternal love about the altar of our common country, the experience, bitter as it is, will not have been in vain.

# FOURTH OF FEBRUARY CONVENTION.*

MR. PRESIDENT—It is a time when all true patriots should carefully consider every proper suggestion having for its object the peace and safety of the country, and we should be very careful that the strong and natural feelings excited by the flagrant acts of rebellion in a very considerable section of the country, do not unduly affect our judgment in looking at the real state of affairs, or in considering remedies that may be proposed. It is morally certain, from the present condition of the country, that a resort to arms for the protection of the Government will be necessary, unless through the influence of wise, judicious and prudent men the intense excitement in the seceding States can be allayed, and thus an opportunity offered for the returning ascendency of reason and judgment.

Whilst no lover of his country will hesitate to perform his full duty in the last resort, yet wisdom

* Delivered in the Senate of Massachusetts, February 4, 1861, upon the Resolves for the appointment of Commissioners to the Virginia Convention of February 4th.

patriotism, and true courage, demand that we shall
not neglect to improve every proper opportunity to
avert such a calamity, and any proposition, from any
quarter, which opens a possible and honorable ave-
nue to avoid precipitating the country into a war
should be entertained by us.  In considering our
duties in regard to the States in open rebellion
even, we should remember the truth which all history demonstrates, and to which I trust this instance is not an exception, that all attempted revolu-
tions and sectional resistance to the laws, undertaken without an adequate cause, are instigated and
controlled by a misguided and excited minority
whose desperation and madness suppress the voice
even of the majority whom they appear to represent, yet who in reality deplore the catastrophe
which in their position they have been powerless to
avert.  I believe a majority of the people of the
States which have undertaken secession, excepting,
perhaps, the people of South Carolina, love the
Union, and look anxiously forward to the time when
the wise action of patriots in other sections will
prove the falsity of the pretexts by which unscrupulous politicians have been enabled to deceive and
mislead their infatuated followers, and allay the excitement; or when, this proving ineffectual, the
strong and paternal arm of the government shall
compel the offenders to an obedience to the laws.

Upon this ground I base my hopes of our beloved

country in the future, and for one, whatever were
the motives which dictated the calling of the Convention of February Fourth, I would respond to the
invitation, hoping, however faintly, that it will legitimately aid in relieving the embarrassments of the
country; and if not, that we shall have the satisfaction in the uncertain future, that in this instance,
at least, we endeavored to leave no duty undone.

The purport of the Resolutions of Virginia have
been misunderstood by many Senators. The first
Resolve is the only one which prescribes the purposes of the Convention, and the only one intended
to give direction to its proceedings. The other
resolutions provide for the election of Commissioners by the several States and express the opinion of Virginia as to the basis upon which an adjustment should be made, but there is nothing in
them mandatory upon the action of the Convention.

The first Resolve is as follows:

*Resolved,*—That on behalf of the Commonwealth of Virginia, an
invitation is hereby extended to all such States, whether slaveholding or non-slaveholding, as are willing to unite with Virginia
in an earnest effort to adjust the present unhappy controversies, in
the spirit in which the Constitution was originally formed, and
consistently with its principles, so as to afford to the people of the
slaveholding States adequate guarantees for the security of their
rights, to appoint Commissioners to meet on the 4th day of February next, in the City of Washington, similar Commissioners appointed by Virginia, to consider and if practicable agree upon
some suitable adjustment.

By this Resolve is clearly intended an adjustment

of existing controversies upon correct principles
and in a proper spirit, and Virginia only claims
that in the adjustment adequate guarantees for the
securities of the rights of the slave States be included.  In this I believe Virginia is right, and no
adjustment can or should be made without such
guarantees.  I believe that Virginia will not, and
under the Resolves cannot, claim that the establishment of such guarantees is the exclusive duty of the
Convention, and that if she does, the Commissioners
from the other States will and should oppose such a
construction.  If this Convention is called in good
faith, with a sincere desire to avert civil dissension,
we may confer a benefit on the country by taking
part in it; and if not thus called, as supposed by
some, then it seems to me it is clearly our duty to
be represented in the convention to see that no mis-
chief is done.  It is time for us to act and act de-
cidedly in the matter.  There has been already too
much delay.  A majority of the free States have already chosen Commissioners, and whatever our own
opinions, we should defer somewhat to the opinions
of the people of our sister States.  Let us not, as
is proposed by the substitute offered, evade the subject—let us meet the question fairly, and determine
unequivocally whether we will or will not take part
in the Convention.

Above all, let Massachusetts show to Virginia
that if she shall prove recreant, that here still ex-

ists a love and devotion for our common country
—that the spirit of liberality and fraternal love
which animated our fathers has not diminished with
time, and that we at least have not forgotten the
sufferings and sacrifices of the founders of the Republic, that the people of these United States and
their posterity forever, might enjoy the blessings of
an enlightened republican civil government.

# RESOLVES ON THE PRESIDENT'S MESSAGE.*

Mr. PRESIDENT:—It is impossible for any of us to exaggerate the importance of the great struggle in which the Government is involved,—important to the entire future of this great people, and not less so to the cause of free institutions throughout the world. The Government of the Union was inaugurated, not without doubt. by our fathers. By a large majority of the people of the old world it was regarded as an experiment, unsupported by the great facts of history. Its failure was predicted. But it was everywhere conceded that, if the system should prove successful,—if this Government, emanating from and depending upon the people, could sustain itself through those great trials and crises which' had been incident to the history of every Government, and in which so many with immense

*Delivered in the Senate of Massachusetts, March 26th, 1862, Resolutions had been reported approving the President's Message of March 6th, to which an amendment was moved by Mr. Thompson of Hampden, approving the entire policy of the President, which amendment, after full discussion, was defeated by a vote of 12 to 22.

central powers had suffered shipwreck, it would mark an era, and would be the signal for an immense and universal advancement in the great cause of liberty and of popular institutions through-out the civilized world.

This Government has survived the exigencies and trials of nearly three-quarters of a century, and many of them of such a character as to lead us, and its friends in the old world, to the belief that its permanency and success were substantially demonstrated.

But in the hour of our greatest prosperity, when the people of the country had come to regard the invincibility of the Government as an established fact, and looked forward to a future of uninterrupted peace and prosperity, we have been suddenly called to meet a crisis of such magnitude and proportions as no one could have anticipated. The only great and untested trial to our Government, under most inauspicious combinations and circumstances, is now upon us, and in our day and generation the great problem of popular institutions is to be settled for at least a century to come. The principles our fathers fought for, the Government they established, the prestige of its unexampled success for so long a time, all stand trembling in the balance; and the responsibility for a right issue, with the interposition of a wise Providence, is upon us,—upon the individuals of the country, upon the citizens in the legislative halls, and the citizens in their homes. No one is exempt from responsibility, and upon individual patriotism, and individual efforts, will history declare the great results of this time.

For months we have waited with the deepest anxiety for tidings of success of our army against the stupendous rebellion. We have recent cause for gratitude that our fellow-citizens in the army are doing their entire duty, and are exhibiting a patriotism and heroism which will, sooner or later, put to an ignominious flight all those arrayed in arms against the Government. But is this all that is to be accomplished? Is the great work of the time finished with the "crushing out" of armed rebellion? Although indispensable, it is but the commencement of the performance of our duties. That finished, we have a country to restore, the Government to be obeyed by a willing people. This result will not depend upon the army, but upon us,— upon the legislators and the people. This is not a war of subjugation. It is a war for and under the Constitution, to protect loyal men oppressed by armed rebellion; and to induce a return to loyalty, and a love and reverence for the Constitution, by showing, as we shall have an opportunity, that cannot and will not be mistaken, that the incendiary statements of the authors of the rebellion were not founded on fact—that they were only plausible pretexts.

This once fully shown, we have a more united and loyal people than we have had for thirty years, and we continue on our great and glorious mission with a power and authority which will more than compensate for all our losses and trials. But if it shall be otherwise,—if the people of this Confederacy, to whom has been entrusted the maintenance of the Government in this great crisis, shall determine to forget the instructions of the fathers,—if they shall be governed by their passions,—if demagogues and the tyranny of party shall usurp the seat of patriotism and true loyalty,—if an unbridled and licentious spirit of recklessness shall madden and impel our people to disregard the guarantees of the Constitution, without which our Government would have never been established, then sir, I see nothing but ruin and disaster in the future.

Let it, sir, be once distinctly understood, that this Government intends to take advantage of the power which this unprecedented state of affairs has entrusted it with, to the subversion of Constitutional rights, and a disregard of constitutional obligations, and the success of our arms will have been in vain. Loyal men of to-day at the South, will see that their rights are violated, and they will strike the heaviest blows for their protection against usurpation. The authors of the rebellion will be able to triumphantly show to their followers, that the specious pretexts which they had used so successfully, if not based upon fact, have resulted in reality, and the last ray of hope for a restoration of the Union will have disappeared.

The President of the United States, from the day of his inauguration to the present time, has proclaimed that the purpose of this war is the restoration of the Union under the Constitution; and under this proclamation, and for the purposes of it, one-half million of our fellow-citizens have volunteered for the war. Every act of the Administration has been consistent with this proclamation, and we are now called upon to express our opinions upon this policy of the Administration; and I beg leave of the Senate, to read from the messages of the President, to show the clear, unqualified, and unmistakable position of the Administration, upon the prosecution of the war.

President Lincoln, in his Inaugural Message, says:

"I have no purpose, directly or indirectly, to interfere with the institution of slavery in the States where it exists. I believe I have no lawful right to do so, and I have no inclination to do so. Those who nominated and elected me, did so with the full knowledge that I had made this, and many similar declarations, and had never recanted them. And, more than this, they placed in the platform for my acceptance, and as a law to themselves and to me, the clear and emphatic resolution which I now read."

"*Resolved* That the maintenance inviolate of the rights of the States, and especially the right of each State to order and control its own domestic institutions, according to its own judgment exclusively, is essential to that balance of power on which the perfection and endurance of our political fabric depend; and we denounce the lawless invasion, by armed force, of the soil of any State or Ter ritory, no matter under what pretext, as among the gravest of crimes."

"I now reiterate these sentiments, and in doing so, I only press upon the public attention, the most conclusive evidence of which the case is susceptible, that the property, peace, and security of no section, are to be in anywise endangered by the now incoming Administration."

In his message to the special session of Congress, July 4th, he says:

"Lest there be some uneasiness in the minds of candid men as to what is to be the course of the Government toward the Southern States after the rebellion shall have been suppressed; the Executive deems it proper to say, it will be his purpose then, as ever, to be guided by the Constitution and the Laws, and that he will probably have no different understanding of the powers and duties of the Federal Government, relatively to the rights of the States and the people under the Constitution, than that expressed in the inaugural address. He desires to preserve the Government, that it may be administered for all, as it was administered by the men who made it."

In his Message to the present session of Congress, in December, the President refers to his two former messages upon this subject, and says, "Nothing now occurs to add or subtract to or from the principles or general purposes stated and expressed in those documents."

In his Message of March 6th, the President recommends to Congress, the adoption of a joint resolution, to the effect that the United States ought to co-operate with any State which may adopt a gradual abolishment of slavery, by giving pecuniary aid for such purpose.

This course has been approved by eminent and conservative statesmen, for many years, and its adoption at the prevent time is specially recommended with the hope that it may induce some of the more Northern slaveholding States to emancipate their slaves, and by so doing, weaken the hopes of the leaders of the insurrection. The resolution contemplates only such action as is strictly within the limits of the Constitution. As the President correctly states in the Message proposing the resolve.—

"Such a proposition on the part of the General Government, se up no claim of a right by Federal authority to interfere with slavery within State limits, referring as it does the absolute control o the subject, in each case, to the State and its people immediately interested. It is proposed as a matter of perfectly free choice with them."

The President further says:

"The point is not that all the States tolerating slavery would soon, if at all, initiate emancipation; but that while the offer is equally made to all, the more Northern shall by such initiation make it certain to the more southern, that in no event will the former ever join the latter in their proposed Confederacy. Initiation' because, in my judgment, gradual and not sudden emancipation is better for all."

These plain and intelligible enunciations of the principles by which the Administration proposed to be guided, met with the approval of the entire people of the loyal States, excepting the class whose basis of operations is outside the Constitution. Men of all parties joined in a patriotic and enthusiastic support of the President upon this distinct line of policy, who would not upon any other; and all who now advocate a different principle of action not only place themselves in opposition to the Administration, but initiate a partisan conflict. This war on the part of the Federal Government, is either for the purpose of restoring and maintaining the supremacy of the Constitution, or for the destruction of it. There is no middle ground. If Senators believe there is such a necessary antagonism between slave labor in one State and free labor in another that they cannot exist together in the future, they should reflect how far this belief justifies an attempt at separation. I believe there is no such antagonism, and the experience of seventy years demonstrates it.

I have not favored the passage of any resolutions by the Legislature upon the conduct of national affairs, and have taken no part in discussions referring to past issues, but these resolutions have been pressed upon us, and we shall be wanting in duty if we remain silent. It is proposed to endorse a portion of the President's policy without reference to the remainder. Such a course, as stated by the Senator from Hampden, Mr. Thompson, in his eloquent remarks, might imply a repudiation of the policy not referred to. All Senators who have spoken, have stated that the people concurred in the entire policy of the President. If this is true, why not express it here. The policy of the President has

been continuous, connected, and consistent, and
should be endorsed as a whole. I believe that it
has been wise, judicious, patriotic. The people believe so. Senators who state that the policy of the
President previous to March 6th is approved by their
constituents, and record their votes against the proposed resolve, will be misunderstood by the people.
We should act with a view to our great responsibilities in the present, with a wise regard to the future,
forgetting all past differences and party divisions.

Our greatest and most holy duty is to sustain the
Government. Every other consideration, however
important, is secondary to it. The evils of slavery
were known to the fathers, as they are known to us,
yet they permitted them, in order that they might
achieve the paramount good of a Government for
this whole people. Let us not assume to be better
or wiser than they were. These evils cannot be
properly relieved by violence, or the arbitrary use
of power. They were not born in a day. They
cannot be cured in a day. Providence will work
out its own great results. This war is for the puri-
fication of the nation, but not by the overthrow of
the Government, or a perversion of any of its fundamental principles. Events sublime, collossal, irre-
sistable, are at work. If we listen, we can hear
their mighty tread. We cannot hasten or aid their
progress by the exercise of extraordinary powers.
Our duty is to exercise faith, patience, in the sup-

port of the Government. Let us do this, and God will protect the right, and in his own way, and in his own good time, will purify us from the wrong.

I know of no way for the restoration of the Union, unless the pilots of the great ship of State shall be guided by the North Star of the Constitution. If this shall be obscured—if we veer to the right hand or the left, we shall find ourselves on a dark and tempestuous ocean, with no haven for safety, our brave soldiers and seamen will have fought to no purpose, the host of noble patriots who have offered up their lives, will have died in vain; and history will record the humiliating truth, that because the sons would not perform the conditions imposed by the fathers, they lost forever, for themselves and their posterity, the most precious inheritance ever bequeathed to a great and prosperous people.

# MARYLAND AND MASSACHUSETTS.*

Mr. President: In this hour of darkness to the Republic, when suspicion and distrust prevail, and the public mind is inflamed with bitter animosities, the slightest occurrence exhibiting good will, the smallest word spoken in kindness by one portion of this people to another, is not without its beneficent effect. The State of Maryland from her position, her business, her social connections, and her institutions, was susceptible to the contagion of Rebellion which had swept like a blight through States on her border. And, maddened by the distractions of the time, by the malaria which was borne upon every breeze from the South, a portion of her people committed a most grievous crime against the Government, by murderous assaults upon loyal citizens hastening to the national capital to protect it from traitor hands which were raised for its destruction; and the victims were men of Massachusetts, our own neighbors, brothers, and sons. Massachusetts

*Delivered in the Senate of Massachusetts, April 22, 1862, upon the Resolve in relation to the Act passed by the General Assembly of Maryland, for the relief of the families of the killed and wounded of Massachusetts, at Baltimore, April 19th, 1861.

felt most deeply the wrong, but she felt it more in sorrow and sadness, than in anger. She mourned that any citizen could raise his hand against that Government which had showered blessings upon all, and in whose perpetuity all her hopes of the future were centred. It was more to her than the loss of her children. And now, when by the patriotic efforts of the sons of Maryland, that noble State is rescued from the vortex of secession into which a portion of her people would have plunged her, she speaks to Massachusetts. She deplores the wrong which some of her citizens committed, and, although as a State she was not responsible for it, she sends from her treasury for the relief of the wounded and the families of the killed. The loyal heart of Maryland has spoken. Massachusetts will respond with a magnanimous spirit. Side by side, and shoulder to shoulder, the sons of Maryland and of Massachusetts are fighting the battles of our country; and when the blessings of peace shall be proclaimed with not a star obliterated from our banner, may all, these experiences contribute to cement these two noble and ancient States in the common brotherhood of the Union.

# ADDRESS AT SALEM.*

Day of hallowed memories—anniversary of our National Independence and of the birth of the Unon—with hearts filled with gratitude we welcome thy return. To God we render devout thanks that we are permitted this inestimable privilege, and that through the thick clouds and darkness which envelope us, we may yet see hope for the future of our beloved country.

It is meet and proper that we should consecrate this day to our country. Its hours are sacred. They connect us with the fathers. In their patriotism and wisdom the people of this great Republic, distracted and embittered by civil dissensions, concur. If we will study their recorded opinions, and become imbued with their spirit, the path of our duty in the momentous future will be plain and intelligible. Read the history of the fathers, of their sufferings and privations, not alone that you may be animated with a feeling of pride at their devo-

---

Delivered before the citizens of Salem, at Mechanic's Hall, July 4th, 1862.

tion, courage and self-sacrifice, but that it may serve
to fix and intensify in your minds the great principles and objects for which they labored.

It was not for power; it was not from motives of
personal ambition or aggrandizement that they suffered; but that they might vindicate the authority
of the people, and be enabled to rear a governmental
fabric, which should be for the permanent happiness
and prosperity of the teeming millions who they fore-
saw must in the future people this immense continent.
It was not for themselves and those with whom they
acted alone, but for their children's children to the
latest generation, that they devoted their lives and
efforts. They were not enthusiasts. Dispassionate
judgment, reason and forethought characterized all
their acts.

The great and sublime object of their lives was constantly before them. Unmoved and serene, they
seemed elevated above the excitements of the time,
and from their majestic height to direct calmly the
progress of events. Temporary disappointments
and disasters, difficulties and dangers, served only to
increase their efforts, and strengthen their faith and
devotion.

Under their guidance, the war of the Revolution
was brought to a successful termination. Their first
purpose was accomplished, and the way opened for
the consummation of the great object of their labors—
the establishment of a government which would

secure to all the nighest blessings of civil liberty,
and bind the people of the thirteen States in a perpetual Union.   Both were in their view indispensable.   A permanent government based upon the will
of the  people was the end to  be attained; and  to
accomplish this  they deemed a union of, the people
of all  the States an absolute  necessity.   They felt
that a liberal government, to  be  perpetual must in-
clude  the  whole—that  it  would  be  impossible for
more than one government to  maintain  a peaceable
existence on  this continent over people of the same
race, civilization and spirit.                      ∡

   It was for  the purpose of establishing such a government ·and  Union  that  the  Convention  of  1787
was held.   It was composed ot  the master spirits of
the  Revolution, and  presided over by  the  immortal
Washington.   The men who had  directed the destinies of the people through the trials and discourage-
ments of an eight years' war, were now called upon
to  undertake  the  most  arduous  and  responsible
duties of the stateman.   But they  shrank not from
the  labor and  responsibility.   They  assembled together, animated by  a common spirit of  patriotism,
and occupied a continuous session of three months, in a
calm  and deliberate consideration and discussion of
the  object for which they  were  convened,  and  the
best mode  of accomplishing it.   It was a stupendous
work.   The opinions and prejudices of  the  people,
sectional  interests,  and existing  powers and  right

were to be harmonized, and a government proposed
which would be accepted by all. These difficulties
were aggravated by the experience they had passed
through. There had existed a Confederation of the
States for five years and a virtual Union for a longer
period. Yet during all this time each State exercised all rights of sovereignty; and even under the
Confederation, no act of the Continental Congress
which it established was effectual until adopted by
the States. Its powers were practically only advi-
sory. Great difficulties had occurred; and the local
power was often invoked against the requirements
of the Union, adding strength to State authority and
zeal to sectional prejudice. These difficulties were
to be encountered and overcome. It required and
called forth a spirit of compromise and concession,
by which alone the great result could be accomplished. The most serious difficulty which embarassed
the Convention was in the disposal of the rights existing in the States. From the experience of the
past, all felt the beneficial results of local legislation
upon the interests of the people; and yet it was
evident that, if a permanent and authoritive government was to be established for the entire people, it
must be clothed with important rights and prerogatives which would essentially abridge the powers of
the States.

In view of the difficulties and embarassments
arising from this state of things, the Convention fi-

nally determined that the proposed new government
should be invested only with such rights and powers
as would be necessary for the general purposes of
government—leaving to the State governments the
entire control of their local institutions and laws,
not conflicting with the positively prescribed objects,
and authority of the General Government; and that
each Government within its prescribed sphere should
be independent of the other.

This system, originating in the necessities of the
time—although recently perverted by a portion of
the people—has had and will continue to have with
our increasing growth a most important influence
upon our prosperity. With a country of such vast
territory, difference of production, interests and
habits, it would be impossible for a central government to legislate satisfactorily for the local requirements of the several sections. But with this reservation of authority in the States to control their domestic institutions and to legislate for their local
purposes, a most important security is afforded
against the conflict of interests which must otherwise
result from the future increase of territory and population.

By this system each State through its Legislature
controls and provides for its own peculiar interests,
and the General Government, representing the unity
of the States, acts as a powerful guardian to protect them in their progress, to decide upon their

conflicting relations, and to accomplish for the general good what it would be impossible for the State
authorities to effect by their separate legislation.
This system of government, embodied in the Constitution of the United States, was proposed by the
Convention to the people of the several States for
ratification or rejection. Conventions were held in
the different States; and finally, after a full discussion, and with a clear understanding of its various
provisions, it was adopted by the people of every
State. George Washington was chosen the first
President under the Constitution. The wheels of
government were set in motion, and the great experiment, as it was called, was put to the test of
practical operation. The effect upon the country
was at once seen and felt. Treaties with foreign
powers were made, commerce increased with wonderful rapidity, manufactures sprung up and agriculture was stimulated. A national credit was established; and, by the close of Washington's administration, we were on the high road to greatness and
prosperity.

We have lived under this Constitution for more
than seventy years. We have, under its wonderful
and beneficient operations, achieved prosperity and
success unparalleled in the history of the world. The
ordinary tests of the strength of a government have
been applied. Difficulties and disputes between
different States have been adjusted, civil disturban-

ces quieted, and the trials and exactions of wars
with foreign powers successfully met. We have
come out of all with renewed strength. We have
laid deep and strong the foundations of literary and
religious institutions. In material prosperity we
have made almost incredible strides. Our commerce
whitens every sea. The stars and stripes, the em-
blem of our national honor and power, wave in every
port. Our manufactures, with a high price for
labor, compete successfully in every market, and, encouraged by them and by the wants of the world,
our agriculture has increased a thousand fold.

All this success has been attained by this great
people under the Government and in the Union as
established by the fathers. From the childhood of
the most aged amongst us, until within a recent period, their continued permanency has never been
reasonably doubted. But within this period, difficulties and dangers beyond the anticipations of any
one have been upon us. From the heights of prosperity and from the enjoyment of a long-continued
peace, we have been precipitated into a conflict of
such colossal proportions as to threaten the very
existence of the Government and the Union.

This conflict has been waged with unremitted
zeal. It has called to the field in defence of the
Government over one-half million of our fellow citizens. Through their heroic efforts, and the wisdom

and prudence of the Federal Administration we have reason to hope that the crisis of rebellion will soon be passed; and that the time is approaching when from the carnage of the battle-field and the excitements of the strife of armies, we shall be called upon to review the ground over which the tornado has swept, and to consider great and important questions —upon the correct decision of which as much as upon the success of our armies, will depend the future continuance of our beloved Union.

These questions deserve your most careful and impartial consideration. At this time, when events are so fast crowding upon us, we cannot determine the entire and inevitable policy of the future. But there are certain great truths and important general principles, which, properly understood and appreciated, will serve to guide us in judging of our duties hereafter. To a brief consideration of some of them I would earnestly urge your attention. In referring to them, I do not propose to appeal to passion or prejudice. They are never safe guides to duty, and are always dangerous in times of great popular excitements. I wish to address myself to your calm reason and judgment. These must be our counsellors, if we would save our country from the perils that threaten it.

In judging of our duties as circumstances shall be developed, it is of primary importance that we understand clearly, appreciate fully, and keep con-

stantly before us, the great object to be attained—
that object is the preservation and continuance of the
Constitution and the Union.

This conflict must result in the supremacy of the
Union or in the overthrow of it. It will be the government of the fathers, or another government or
governments to be hereafter established. It will be
the Constitution and the Union in their integrity, or
the Constitution and the Union in ruins.

Let us not be deceived—let us not deceive ourselves. The Constitution is the fundamental law
which is to govern and control us. From it the government and the Union have their legal existence.
It confers rights and privileges, and imposes duties
and obligations. The former must be fairly permitted, and the latter fairly performed, or the Constitution is inoperative. If the performance of these
duties and obligations is successfully resisted by the
people of any State or section, a revolution in that
State or section is achieved; and the natural tendency is to extend revolution to other States and
sections until the prestige and authority of the government will have become extinct. If, on the other
hand, the General Government, in obedience to the
demands of the majority, shall proceed to deprive the
people of any State or section of their rights and
privileges under the Constitution, except so far as
the necessities of the government may require, for
its preservation, their temporary supension or abridge-

ment, it will be a usurpation of power, revolutionary, and destructive of the Constitution.

The Government and the Union can only exist and be respected by a strict adherence to the Constitution. We must be guided by it, if we hope for peace, safety and union hereafter. It will survive the present conflict invested with increased strength and authority, or it will suffer wounds which will sooner or later prove mortal.

If we favor reconstruction, that presupposes dissolution. If we would proclaim universal emancipation of slaves in the States, we can only do it by trampling upon the Constitution, which leaves the entire and exclusive control of the subject to the respective States. If we determine to conquer, and hold as subjugated, the people of great States or sections, we can find no authority in the letter or spirit of the Constitution for the act.

The exercise of powers indispensable for the maintenance of the Government, in the absence of prescribed law, is not in violation of the Constitution. In a case like the present it is made the duty of the President, by the Constitution, to suppress rebellion; the means were in his hands, and it was incumbent on him to employ those means honestly and fairly, for the purpose of such suppression. The right and duty are based upon the clearly recognized law of self-preservation. Yet this law has well defined imits. The employment of the means is limited by .

the necessity. Although it imposes upon the President the duty of employing such power as shall be sufficient to meet the necessity—or, in the words of President Lincoln, "inevitable necessity"—yet it forbids his using more than is necessary, or preverting the power for any other purpose. It imposes upon the head of the nation the exercise of the highest discretion; and he undertakes, with no written law to guide him, a most responsible duty, when he employs the means in his hands for the suppression of a rebellion threatening the existence of the Government; and he would be guilty of the grossest wrong, if, under the pretext of necessity, he should invoke powers not indispensable, or means for other objects not required by the exigency. The greater the discretionary power, the greater the responsibility that exists for a proper and prudent application and employment of it.

And it is to us a cause of great satisfaction that the Chief Executive of the Union, in the trying and perplexing emergencies in which the Government has been placed, has exhibited such patriotism, sound wisdom and discretion in the exercise of this power, as to meet the approval of all loyal citizens.

Believing, then, that all true patriots concur in the conviction that the great object of our efforts is the maintenance of the Constitution inviolate, it becomes our duty to do everything consistent with honor to promote that object. To this end, we must at all sacrifices put down armed rebellion. We must scatter the armies of the rebels, and satisfy the people of the rebellious States that the power of the General Government, wherever restored, will be forever after maintained. This being done, our next duty is to secure obedience to the government by a willing people. The first is to be effected through the instrumentality of the army and navy; and the next through the instrumentality of the people. For the successful accomplishment of both, it is necessary that it be distinctly understood what the policy of the Government will be towards those who have rebelled against its authority.

If it shall be proclaimed that the purpose of the Government is to hold the so-called seceded States as subjugated and tributary provinces; or that the masses of the people, upon the acknowledgement of their errors, are to be stripped of their property and to forfeit their rights under the Constitution, we cannot hope for a speedy termination of the war. We may have success on the battle-field, but we cannot conquer a peace. History should teach us the Herculean task a government undertakes, which would hold, impoverished and disfranchised, a population so large as that of the South, and occupying such a vast extent of territory.

The practical difficulties of such a course, even if such were within our rightful discretion, should be sufficient to compel us to reflection, without considering further its inconsistency with the great principles of equality, upon which our institutions are based.

The necessity which exists for the temporary exercise of authority by officers appointed by the President, in States from which the armies of the rebels have been expelled, does not conflict with these views. These officers are not placed in authority for the purpose of compelling the people to submit to deprivations of their rights and property, but as substitutes for the civil authorities who have abdicated, and for the purpose of maintaining the laws and protecting the rights and property of the people, until they shall elect loyal rulers to take their places.

A government of a civilized people can only hope for a return of its rebellious citizens to loyalty, obedience and respect, through the adoption of a lenient and forgiving policy toward the masses. This is not only a political necessity, but consistent with that charitable and merciful spirit which should ever animate a civilized and Christian government. Upon this all publicists agree. It is the policy laid down by the law of nations. The force of this law has been incidentally stated by one of our Senators in Congress, in the discussion of another topic; he says international law, "when justly and authoritatively settled, becomes a safeguard of peace and a landmark of civilization. It constitutes a part of that code which is the supreme law, above all municipal laws, binding the whole commonwealth of nations."

Vattel, in his great work upon international law, says: "Subjects rising against their prince without cause deserve severe punishments; yet here the number of delinquents calls for the sovereign's clemency. Shall he depopulate a city or desolate a province in punishing their rebellion? Such a chastisement, however just in itself, becomes a cruelty when extended to so great a number of persons." And further—"As for penalties, let them be reserved for the authors of the rebellion, for those incendiaries who incite the people to revolt."

If a rebellious people, when brought within the power of the government, are, for their errors, to be deprived of their rights, immunities and property, they will forever after entertain sentiments of hostility, which will manifest themselves against the government upon every occasion. They will continually feel their humiliation and deprivations, and can never be faithful citizens. Whereas, if those who have been induced to commit wrongs against their government are forgiven their offences, the magnanimity of the act operates to increase and strengthen their returning sentiments of loyalty.

This rule, in its policy and mercy, does not extend to the leaders of the rebellion. Few in number, the authorities can deal with them differently. Their crime is deeper. Their punishment, upon conviction

under the laws of the land, will be a just retribution
to them, and will afford an example in the future.
These general principles, so necessary in their application, so wise and merciful in their operations, are
acknowledged by all as obligatory upon our government.

But, with this acknowledgement upon their lips,
there are individuals who refuse that these principles shall be applied to the relation which exist between the master and his slaves, in the rebellious
States. They claim that the slaves of all in rebellion, of the leaders and the masses alike, shall be
freed. This claim is in direct violation of these
principles. If it is necessary to a voluntary return,
that the masses shall be reinstated in their rights
under the Constitution, and that their property shall
not be confiscated, will not such a course as is proposed, absolutely prevent their return? Can it
have any other effect upon them than to keep alive
feelings of enmity toward the Government, instead
of that respect and love which is indispensable to
make them faithful citizens? It is most important
to understand the value which they attach to the
right of which you would deprive them, to compre-
hend the effect of the act upon their minds. The
importance to them is the measure of its effect. The
right is one they estimate of the highest value;
and there is no right connected with property, with
the strong feeling engendered upon the subject, of

which they are more tenacious or sensitive. I believe that if such an innovation upon the principles, which it is admitted should control the action of the Government, is adopted, there can be no hope of a voluntary return. The conflict will result in successful revolution, abject subjugation or utter extermination. Those who propose this course attempt to justify it upon the ground that it is necessary for the suppression of the rebellion. But, as I have before stated, there must exist an absolute necessity in order to justify the use of powers not prescribed by the laws. It is not sufficient that a certain course, or the adoption of certain means, will aid in putting down the rebellion—that they will strengthen the hands of the government—or that, through their influence, the conflict may be brought to a speedy conclusion. There must exist an inevitable necessity, one which the calm judgment of the future will acknowledge, to justify the use of any such extraordinary powers. With the immense numerical superiority of our population, our vast resources, and great success in the past, can it be said that our government is now under such a necessity for self-preservation, that it must interfere with important constitutional rights for its relief? And if such necessity should exist, the government must use such means only as are useful and appropriate to meet it. The fact that there exists an exigency which cannot be relieved through the means and modes prescribed

by law, does not authorize the government recklessly
to interfere with rights irrespective of the effect.   It
must be reasonably assured that a proposed course
will materially aid in overcoming the impending
necessity, and that it is adapted to that end.   The
President has thus far seen no exigency which required the exercise of the proposed power.   None
such exists, and there is little reason to anticipate
that any will exist in the future.   If any such necessity shall arise, it will result from such a state of
facts as to satisfy all reasonable loyal men, both
North and South; and they will cheerfully acquiesce
in the exercise of the necessary power.

If the Government is under the necessity of employing extraordinary powers, it is very evident that,
under present circumstances, an attempt to free the
slaves of all in rebellion would not aid the Government.   A proclamation for the purpose could have
no effect in advance of our military power.   It could
hardly secure the freedom of a single slave who is
not liberated as a necessity, with the progress of the
Federal army.   For material aid, such a proclamation would be but of paper strength.   But, on the
other hand, such a proclamation would aggravate
the difficulties to be overcome, and operate most dis-
asterously upon the great object for which we are
striving.   It would encourage the masses in resistance, who have taken up arms in the belief that the
object of the Government is to force emancipation

upon the States; and would dispel the ray of hope
from the hearts of those in the South who have
looked to the eventual restoration of the Union for
relief from the present reign of terror. And the
effect of such a proclamation, unless justified by necessity, would operate most injuriously upon the people of Delware, Maryland, Missouri and Kentucky.
They would see that their rights are involved; and
that, if the Government should unjustifiably interfere
with slavery in the rebellious States, there would be
but little hope in the future for security to slavery
in their own States. These people are entitled to
our highest consideration. By the patriotic and
strenuous efforts of these men, those great States
have been saved from the vortex of secession, and
held true to the Constitution and the Union; and a
large portion of them are slaveholders. It was
stated in Congress, by one of the Representatives
from Kentucky, that "it appears by the assessor's
books of that State, that over eighty per cent of the
slaves there, are owned by Union men, whose blood
has been shed upon every battle-field since Kentucky
entered this war." Without the co-operation of
these States, we might well despair of the cause of
the Union; and, with them, under a wise policy,
there can be no permanent separation. Their interests, to a large extent, were with the seceding
States, but their duty was to the Government to
which they owed allegiance; and they followed the

path of their duty.   And they have shown their loyalty through their sufferings.   If there are any men in the country whom I especially honor, they are the noble and self-sacrificing patriots of the Border States.   Their homes have been desolated and their fields devastated, but they have stood firm by the Constitution.   Their rights and their interests should be sacred to the loyal people of the Union.

There is nothing connected with the conduct of the war, from which more mischievous results will follow, than from an unjustifiable interference with slavery in the States.

The effect of the wrongful exercise of power, upon those who are its victims, may be illustrated by the familiar instance of the action of the civil authorities in staying the spread of a conflagration in a large city.   If necessary for the purpose, the municipal officers may destroy buildings in advance of the devouring element.   They are justified from the existence of an overwhelming necessity; and the public cheerfully acquiesce.   But if, instead of demolishing buildings near to the conflagration, they should destroy others at a distance from the scene of danger, and to which there is no apparent probability the flames can extend, the act cannot be justified; and the authorities will be amenable.   And if, in addition, the owners of the buildings entertain the belief, with or without sufficient cause, that their destruction had been long desired by the authoritise,

for other and distinct purposes, they would connect
such motive with the act, and regard it as a gross
violation of their rights. The fact that they are destroyed under the mere pretext of necessity, instead·
of diminishing, will only add to their resentment.

It is plain that, under existing circumstances, to
declare the emancipation of the slaves of all in rebellion, could have no other influence than to prevent
the accomplishment of our object—obedience to the
Government by a willing people.

It is sufficient for us to provide for the great exigencies of the present, with an anxious effort so to
direct events, as to accomplish the great result, upon
the expediency, propriety and right of which, there
should exist no difference of opinion among loyal
men.

Another ground, upon which such interference
with slavery is attempted to be justified, is that of
political necessity. The statement is, that the Union will not hereafter be safe if slavery is permitted
in the States. This ground has no foundation upon
any possible legitimate principle. Even if it were
true that there existed lawfully under the Constitution, institutions and systems, from which danger
in the future is to be apprehended, it would give no
authority to the people to remove them by the lay-
ing of violent hands on the Constitution. The Constitution provides for its own amendment, and no
exigencies of political necessity can justify the ac

complishment of a desired change, except through the mode provided in the instrument itself. Such an attempt would be clearly and unqualifiedly revolutionary.

But it may be useful to look further, and to enquire if there is any such danger to our Government in the future, from the existence of slavery, as to demand a change through the mode established by the Constitution.

There is nothing in the relation of slavery to our material prosperity which is dangerous. The fact that all of the cotton and tobacco of the country is cultivated by slave labor is not dangerous to the Government, and does not injuriously affect the character of free labor upon other productions, in other sections. The effect of permitting slave labor is most injurious to free labor in the same State and society, but not beyond it. Further, if free labor can control, in any State in which the great staples now cultivated by slave labor are produced, free labor, instead of being prejudiced, will be benefitted by the competition. Upon the same product, the economy of free labor will drive slave labor from the field; and if a great cotton growing State, like Texas for example, could be converted to free labor—to which its population and events seem fast compelling it—the result would be the abandonment, within no great length of time, of slave labor in every Gulf State. It would quietly and gradually yield to the competition; and the people would find their best interests subserved in the substitution of free labor.

The evils of slavery, the fathers of the country knew and felt; yet the system was so strongly sustained by the sentiment of the people in the States where it existed, that they could not demand its abandonment without thereby preventing the establishment of the Union. Although comparatively stronger then than now—as it existed in a majority of the States—they voluntarily left it where the Constitution found it—under the control and to the responsibility of the respective States, hoping that circumstances and the highest interests of the people themselves would, sooner or later, put it in the way of ultimate extinction. The people of the North have believed that, if its extention into future States could be prohibited, it would gradually come to a termination, and, upon the question of such extension, there has been severe political strife. This rebellion has forever settled it in favor of freedom. All the territory of the country has, by a recent vote of Congress, been forever dedicated to free labor; and no future legislation or power can wrest it from the freemen who will people it at the close of the war.

Congress has also, upon the recommendation of the President, passed a resolve to the effect that the General Government will render pecuniary aid to any State which shall determine upon the emancipation of its slaves, and with the march of our armies into the rebellious States, slavery, from necessity has received the severest blow.

These important results have been lawfully achieved. They follow legitimately from the state of affairs caused by the rebellion. Slavery precipitated, by its friends, has received a blow from which it can never recover. Events, more effectual than arbitrary and unauthorized power will gradually and peaceably, but surely dispose of it. With these great and significant facts before our eyes, God save us from the suicidal act of precipitating slavery and the Union into one common grave. Fellow-citizens, judge of this carefully. Be not allured by the siren song of those who would persuade you to seek by rash and forcible means to escape possible evils, by plunging into dangers from which there can be no return.

I entertain now, as I have ever entertained the clearest convictions of the evils of slavery, and I look forward with hope to the day when it will be peaceably and wholly removed from our midst. But strong as are these convictions and earnest as are these hopes, I have never learned to weigh in the balance, the importance of its immediate removal against the life of this great Government.

For the restoration of the Union in its integrity, there is only one certain path. It may lead over rough mountains, across deep abysses, and by the edge of fearful precipices, but it is the only path to safety and peace. Any other course will be revolu- tionary and destructive of the Constitution. Any other course must result in a necessity for recon- struction. Does the word reconstruction convey no terror to the American mind? It is not and cannot be a peaceable and insensible transition from the present to the future Government.

Absolute destruction must precede reconstruction and with it must come anarchy, confusion, fierce civil dissensions at home, and all the long and dis- astrous train of evils to which misguided and uncon- trolled human passions lead. Twenty millions of people, with diversity of interests. dispositions and political opinions,—which, under our beneficent sys- tem, have co-operated so harmoniously that the very diversity imparted additional strength and se- curity — will be absolved from their reciprocal obli- gations. Disintegration will ensue; and the people will be called upon to establish a new government. Will no conflicts of interests spring up? Will there be no jealousies between the East and the West, between New England and the great States border- ing upon the seceded section? Will there be no difficulty in establishing a basis for the payment of the debt of the old Government — or the whole of it being due to the East, will an attempt be made to repudiate it? Will there be no resentments

D

arising from divided opinions upon the policy which
had made reconstruction necessary ?    Will there not
be innumerable causes and pretexts for variance ?
The real danger from such a state of things cannot
be exaggerated.   In our own history we learn the
difficulty of establishing a government by the people,
even after a long experience which satisfied all of its
necessity.   We know with what anxiety the subject
was considered by the people — with what faithful-
ness, ability and patriotism it was discussed by the
great men of the day. the length of time required
to accomplish the adoption of the Constitution, and
that the fact of its final adoption was regarded as
almost a miracle.

The appeal of Alexander Hamilton to the American people in behalf of the present Constitution.
when, although it had been adopted by seven of the
States, apprehensions were felt that it might not be
by all — shows the deep anxiety that great and
patriotic statesman felt in the result.   It is in the
last number of the *Federalist*.   He said : " It may
be in me a defect of political fortitude, but I acknowledge that I cannot entertain an equal tranquility with those who affect to treat the danger of
a longer continuance in our present situation as
imaginary.   A *nation* without a *national government*
is an awful spectacle.   The establishment of a Constitution, in time of profound peace, by the voluntary
consent of a whole people, is a prodigy, to the con-

templation of which I look forward with trembling anxiety. In so arduous an enterprise, I can reconcile it to no rules of prudence to let go the hold we now have upon seven out of the thirteen States, and after having passed over so considerable a part of the ground, to recommence the course. I dread the more the consequences of new attempts, because I *know* that *powerful* individuals, in this and in other States, are enemies to a general national government in every possible shape."

These words will apply with great force to our position if we shall be called upon to reconstruct the government; and the apprehensions will be intensified from the fact that it is a call to reconstruct, with the discouraging reflection that the new government is to succeed the best government which ever existed on the face of the globe, and which had been unnecessarily and capriciously thrown away.

But the important question remains to be considered. Will the people of the States in rebellion, after the power of the Government has been successfully manifested, and with the exercise of a rightful policy, voluntarily return to their allegiance?

Our expectations upon this question will be materially affected by an understanding of the causes of the rebellion. If an intelligent people have taken up arms against their Government to effect a revolution from an adequate cause, it is useless to hope for their return to loyalty, until that cause has been removed by the Government. If, on the other hand, a revolt has been instigated and overt acts of rebellion committed, without an adequate cause, we may reasonably hope for a return to loyalty when, after failure of armed resistance, time has been given for calm reflection. The slaveholders and the non-slaveholding whites, who took an early and active part in the rebellion, were governed by the belief that the National Administration had determined to pervert the powers of the government to compel emancipation of slaves in the States. The slaveholders were induced to action for the protection of their material interests; and the non-slaveholding population, which constituted by far the larger portion, from dislike of the negro, and a belief that he was to be emancipated and placed on an equality with themselves. These opinions were strengthened through the incendiary eloquence of their political leaders, upon whom the people of the South have ever placed great reliance.

Without this belief, these various classes could not have been induced to the course they adopted. History teaches us that masses of men are not easily moved to take up arms against their government; and, in the words of the Declaration of Independence, which have just been read, "all experience, hath shown that mankind are more disposed to suffer, while evils are sufferable, than to right themselves by abolishing the forms to which they were accustomed. "

They may have acted upon a mistaken belief. But as a motive to action, a mistaken conviction of the existence of a fact is as influential as if the fact itself existed.

I believe it is true that a majority of the people in most, if not all of the rebellious States, even to the hour of the passage of their acts of secession, were loyal; and that a large portion of them were the land-holders. And I believe it is also true that a very large portion of them have since, more or less actively, sustained the rebellion. The reasons and motives which affected this change well deserve our consideration. A portion of this class sincerely believed in the doctrine that a State has a right to secede; and although they preferred that the Union should be maintained, yet they felt bound by the action of their State, and believed that it was their duty to support it, even against their individual convictions of its inexpediency.

Another portion, with the same preferences, believed that from what had been accomplished a separation of the States was inevitable; and, with this conviction, they deemed that the general good of all would be best promoted by its speedy accomplishment. They saw the utter futility, in their position, of making any attempt to resist the storm of rebellion; and concluded that a dissolution of the

Union and the chances of establishing new govern ments, were to be preferred to fierce and lasting civil dissensions at home. May we not be too censorious in judging of the decisions and acts of these men? We must remember the position in which they were placed, the fact that the entire power of their own States, and of neighboring States, was exerted in favor of revolution; and that all interference of the general Government was forcibly and effectually excluded.

Another portion was undoubtedly compelled to a decision through fear. The acts of confiscation and other stringent laws enacted against the property and persons of those who should oppose the revolutionary policy, forced them to compliance.

Those who enlisted in the cause of rebellion from other motives than the wish to break up the Union, may be more readily won back to allegiance. They will see, with the advance of our victorious armies that they have acted upon erroneous views, and with mistaken opinions of the result. May we not reasonably hope to see the day when they will rejoice with us in the accomplished salvation of our common country?

All this is not the work of a day. It will call for time, patience, perseverance, labor. But, if, in the end, through the dark shadows which surround us we can see peace and safety, and a strengthened and confirmed Union, it will be to us all a sufficient reward for our efforts.

God disciplines nations as he does individuals. It is only through trials, temptations and dangers that we are strengthened and exalted. May it not be that, in His infinite wisdom, He has sent this sore trial upon us to discipline our hearts, to chasten our pride, to test our patience and forbearance, to increase our faith and hope — and above all, to. manifest to the people of this great nation His infinite power.

But, fellow citizens, time admonishes me that I may weary your patience. Appreciating, as I humbly trust, somewhat, the magnitude of the dangers which threaten our beloved country, and feeling as I do the conviction, that unless the American mind shall be inspired with prudence and wisdom, the return of this day may witness a permanently divided union and a distracted people — that within that brief period this great Government, set as a light to the world, may be extinguished forever — I cannot close without solemnly adjuring each citizen within the sound of my voice, to enquire anxiously for himself what course he can pursue which will best subserve the maintenance of the Constitution and the restoration of the Union, in the preservation and integrity of which are centred all our precious hopes of the future.

Divest your minds of the passions and resentments of the time. It is no easy task. Bury with the dead all party ambition and jealousies. The spirit of party is now a genius of evil. Look only at your bleeding country, that you may be animated with the single purpose of saving it from its perils. The people of this country can save it. What nobler cause can engage your efforts? It is above every other earthly consideration. Pride and selfishness should bow before the awful majesty of the occasion. What is the temporary success or promotion of an individual compared with his interest and that of his children in the perpetuation of American institutions. Learn a lesson from the noble men who are fighting our battles. They count their lives as nothing for the protection of the Government. Can we not, emulating their spirit, yield something? Can we not cast prejudice and passion a burning and acceptable sacrifice, upon the altar of our country?

Fellow-citizens, great is the responsibility which rests upon us of this generation. To our wisdom, reason and patriotism has Providence submitted the question of the future existence of the great American system, for a final decision. The life of this great nation is in the hands of the people. Will you save it? I appeal to your dearest and highest interests. I appeal to you in behalf of the millions in other lands, who are looking with the intensest, interest upon the fortunes of this great struggle. I call upon you, in behalf of a great posterity, to rise to the terrible importance of the hour.

I beseech of you all to determine that, God help-
ing, you will, under the guidance of the great and
glorious principles of the Civil and Christian law,
do what you can to bring back to a common love
and allegiance, this great and unhappy people.

# SPEECH AT BOSTON.*

The excitements of the annual canvass have passed with the election, and it is now a peculiarly fitting time to consider dispassionately the actual condition and exigencies of the country, and to counsel together upon our duties in the great and momentous future. The country has been now for nearly three years contending with a colossal rebellion. The sacrifice of blood and treasure, and the destruction of resources in this struggle, are almost, if not entirely, unprecedented in the history of the civilized world. Within that brief period of time we have sent to the field of carnage nearly one and a half million of our chosen youth, a majority of whom to-day lie buried beneath the soil of distant battle-fields, languish in hospitals, or are returned, enfeebled and incapacitated for labor.

We have expended nearly two thousand millions of dollars of treasure. A large portion of the country has been swept as by the besom of destruc-

* Delivered before the Constitutional Democratic Club, Boston, November 4, 1863.

tion. Whole States almost have been devastated.
Business, even in the most prosperous portion of the
country, has been forced from its natural channels,
and turned principally to provide for the necessities
occasioned in the prosecution of the war, and has
been feeding on the credit of the country, for the
support of which the labor and energies of the people must be taxed for generations to come—and
the end is not yet.

This state of affairs calls for the most anxious
and careful consideration, and a most thorough and
impartial discussion of the various important questions connected with the struggle, to the end that
the people may concur in, and require the adoption
of such measures as will accomplish the settlement
of our National difficulties, and a return of the blessings of peace, within some appreciable period.

. It is our duty, in considering these great and important questions, to discard, so far as we may be
able, all passion, animosity and partizan bitterness,
and to appeal to the judgment and the reason alone.
True patriots can now look only to the interests of
the country. All mere party considerations are but
dust in the balance, when compared with the gigantic issues in which are involved the life and the death
of the Union. Under our institutions the people
can only unite in the expression of their opinions
upon these great issues through political organiza
tions, and it is for this purpose now that they are

or should be, of any value.    The object of the people in support of the Government is to restore our
country, so far as it may be done, to its former condition, through the suppression of the force which is
employed against it, and by allaying the animosities
which have for the time estranged and divided the
people of the country.    It is indispensable that both
these purposes be accomplished, if the Constitution
is to be continued and the Union restored.    These
results can be accomplished only through the adoption and execution of a wise, comprehensive and patriotic policy.    Abstract dogmas, speculative theories, partizan intensity and zeal, cannot compass this
end.    It must be effected, if at all, through policy,
through the employment of such means, compatable
with law and honor, as shall under the circumstances be best adapted for the accomplishment of the
desired result.    What we can honorably and legitimately do, that will most effectually and speedily
suppress the force opposed to the government and
restore the lost affections of the people, it is our first
and  highest  duty  to  do.    No  great  rebellion
was ever undertaken, that did not originate either
in the oppression of the government, or in imaginary grievances, believed to be real by the masses of
those who rebelled.    No such rebellion as we are
called upon to meet was ever undertaken and perse-
vered in with such an intensity by any civilized people, through mere recklessness, or the influence of

ambitious leaders alone. It is our duty, then, to
look for the cause of the rebellion, for that which
has given strength and vitality to the force employed. If we shall find that any actual grievance was
the cause of the insurrection, then it is our duty, in
accordance with the policy pursued by civilized nations, to relieve it; and if the grievance is only
imaginary — " a phantom, " the same policy demands
of us that we should attempt to remove and dispel
the delusion. This is necessary, not only to regain
the confidence and affections of the people in the end,
but indispensable for the purpose of so weakening
the strength of the force which sustains the rebellion, that it may be overcome by the government.

A people thoroughly united in support of a rebellion, can never be conquered and made obedient and
faithful subjects or citizens, through the application
of force alone; and so long as force is employed
against a united people, without conciliation, it will
fail of its object, and tend only to confirm the intensity of the spirit of resistance.

The immediate cause of the rebellion was perfectly well understood by the President, by Congress
and by the people, at the time of the breaking out
of the war. The subject had been for months discussed in Congress and before the people, and there
was no misconception or misunderstanding in regard
to it. The President appreciating it fully, expressed
it in clear and emphatic language in his inaugural

message, March 4, 1861. He said:

"Apprehension seems to exist among the people of the Southern States, that by the accession of a Republican Administration, their property, their peace, and their personal security are to be endangered."

This was the sole immediate cause of the disturbed feeling that agitated the South and ominously threatened the peace and the integrity of the country. It was not the power of leaders, it was not recklessness in the people, it was not a spirit of aggression on the part of the South that endangered the peace of the country, but an apprehension — a real actual fear among the people of the South. that the new Administration, based upon principles antagonistic to their institutions, controlled by men who had declared a purpose to illegally interfere with the rights of the people of the Southern States, and succeeding to power by a purely sectional vote, intended to strike at their property, their peace and their personal security. This every man in the country knew was the sole immediate cause from which the peace of the country was endangered, and every man felt that if this apprehension could be relieved, the country would be composed. Conservative men of both sections made every effort to remove these apprehensions and avert the war. Mr Crittenden, a man in whose wisdom, disinterestedness and loyalty, no one doubted, presented to Congress, early in the winter, a series of resolutions intended to remove these apprehensions. Jefferson Davis, even, assented to the statement of their effect, and approved of their passage for the purpose of preventing war; but the leaders of the Republican party refused to accept them. The cause was not removed, conciliation was declined to be offered, and war followed.

The President, in his inaugural message, proposed conciliation. He stated the aprehensions of the people of the South. solemnly affirmed that he had no purpose, directly or indirectly, to interfere with the institution of slavery in the States where it exists and that he had no lawful right nor inclination thus to interfere. He referred to his statements in the past, the resolution of the Chicago platform on the subject, and in the strongest and most convincing language, assured the people that the property, peace and security of no section were to be in anywise endangered by the incoming Administration. These assurances had great influence upon a large portion of the people of the South, but the refusal of the Republicans in Congress, to pledge their party to non-interference, in their refusal to pass the Crittenden resolutions, had already rendered it morally certain, that open rupture could not be avoided. Those men at the South, who were relieved of their apprehensions through the patriotic assurances of the President, were sustained through the terrible pressure which the commencement of the war brought upon their whole section by the hope that, through his wisdom and patriotism, the rebellion would be speedily suppressed, and the lost affections of the people restored; and the President had the satisfaction of stating to Congress, in his message in July, nearly three months after the attack on Fort Sumter, that "It may well be questioned, whether there is to-day a majority of the legally qualified voters of any State, except, perhaps, South Carolina in favor of disunion. There is much reason to believe that the Union men are the majority, in many, if not in every one of the so-called seceded States."

The effect of the President's announcement of the policy that would govern him, was still more influential upon the people of the North. It united the whole people in a most cordial and enthusiastic support of the Administration for the vigorous prosecution of the war against armed rebellion, with the confidence that under a wise management, it could soon be suppressed and the Union restored to peace through the aid of the Unionists of the South. So influential was this sentiment of the people, that Congress, immediately after the battle of Bull Run, passed, with almost entire unanimity, the Crittenden resolves. Under this policy, in the winter and spring following, successful efforts were made against the rebellion in all quarters. The rebels themselves were dismayed at their defeats; and the Union men looked forward to an early day when they could again see the old stars and stripes wave over their

heads. Richmond alone remained to be taken. Although within our grasp, it was not taken,
and history will not attribute the failure to the want
of bravery in our men, or of generalship in that
noble military chieftain who led his forces unsustain-
ed, within sight of the spires of the Confederate
capital.

If the administration had properly supported Gen.
McClellan, Richmond would have fallen, the back
bone of the rebellion would have been broken, and
the Union restored through the vote of a majority of
the people of the South, who had never sympathized
with the rebellion.

But whilst our brave men were fighting armed rebellion under the declared policy of the President
and Congress, mischievous and zealous politicians
were plotting the overthrow of the policy, and advo-
cating an antagonistic and partisan system of operations against the insurgents. They did not desire
reconciliation through conciliation, and feared above
all things the return of the people of the South to
allegiance and a participation in the Government, as
they knew it would prove the death knell to their
party organization. They saw it was indispensable
for their future success to repudiate the real cause
of the war, and to attribute it to such a cause as
would aid them in their partisan designs. The theory they promulgated was, that the apprehension of
the people of the South that their peace, property

and security would be endangered by the new Administration, did not cause the national disturbance, but that the existence of slavery was the sole cause of it — that in itself slavery is such an antagonistic and disturbing element, that the only solution of our present difficulties, and our only hope of peace in the future, is from the overthrow and extinction of it; and that consequently, instead of attempting conciliation, the war should be directed to the forcible overthrow of the system. This policy was initiated by the introduction into Congress and subsequent passage of the confiscation act, and finally adopted by the President, September, 1862, and under it, substantially, the war has been prosecuted from that time to the present. The destructive character of this policy, and the fallacy on which it is based, are apparent to every unprejudiced mind. Yet, the fact that it has been adopted to govern in the prosecution of the war, and that it is the basis of the platform of the Administration party, and accepted by many without consideration, under the pressure of partisan influences, demands an examination of it which it otherwise would not deserve.

If it shall be conceded for the moment, that the authors of the new policy are correct in their statement that slavery, as it legally exists under the Constitution, was not only the sole cause of the war, but that it is intrinsically so disturbing an element, that so long as it exists, this people can never live together in the Union in peace, does it legally or morally justify their sequence, that therefore, it should be forcibly destroyed, without the consent of the people, who, under the Constitution, have the exclusive control of it? If their statement is correct, the only just and logical sequence is, that if the people of the South cannot be induced voluntarily to abandon it then that we should at once consent to a separation of the Union. Upon their statement of facts, we have no legal or moral right to compel a change, and we assume a fearful responsibility, if we proceed to sacrifice life, treasure and national resources for the accomplishment of such an unjust and illegal purpose. What would be thought in a community, of a firm which should undertake by force to prevent one of its members from doing a private business, which it was agreed. in the partnership bond he might do, merely upon the ground that the strict exercise of the privilege operated more injuriously and destructively upon the business of the firm than it was anticipated it would when the partnership was created? The only remedy in such a case would be, if the partner would not voluntarily yield the privilege, to cancel the bond and dissolve the partnership. Should any other rule control in a government of the people?

If the statement of the authors of the new policy is correct, I know of no reason why they should not concur in the demands of the South.

But this statement is not correct, and it is perhaps not strange that in a time of such intense excitement, members of the Republican party should willingly and without examination accept a theory in itself plausible but ill-founded, which harmonizes with their partisan interests and is consistent with their party shibboleth. Slavery was in no sense the cause of the war. The fact that labor is performed in one State of the Union by slaves, and in another by free men, occasions no "irrepressible conflict." This the author of the term admitted in a speech delivered just before the commencement of the war. The fact furnishes no antagonism which is destructive of the national life. For one hundred years before the adoption of the Constitution, the labor in one part of the country was performed by slaves, and in another principally by free men, and no antagonism was produced or dreamed of. In the convention which framed the Constitution there were men from both sections who openly deplored the fact that slavery existed, and who opposed the continuance of the slave trade, yet there was not one who suggested that there was any intrinsic antagonism in the system, which could endanger the government they were creating; and upon the test question on the subject, the provision for the rendition of fugitives, there was not one dissenting vote. For forty years after the adoption of the Constitution, we lived together in the Union, a portion of the

States slave and a portion free, not only without any antagonism exhibiting itself, but without any being suggested. The only civil disturbance of magnitude which has threatened us in the past, was in South Carolina, on the subject of the tariff alone. But the last thirty years has witnessed a great political strife on the subject of slavery. It commenced with the organization of the anti-slavery society in 1833. This was formed not upon the ground that slavery was dangerous to the National Government, but purely upon the moral questions arising out of it. From that time to the present, able and eloquent men and women have addressed meetings in every village of the North, in which they denounced the people of the South as a barbarous and unchristian race, not fit to be associated under the same government with the people of the North. Fanatical philanthropists, excited upon the subject, demanded a separation of the Union, and fanatical clergymen called for a separation of the church. This excited a counter irritation at the South. The excitement there was stronger, as it was connected with their most important material interests. The inevitable result was the rank growth of a most bitter animosity and hatred between the people of the two sections. Demagogues in both sections turned the excitement to their own partisan purposes. Stringent legislation in South Carolina and other Southern States upon the subject of free negroes followed.

The North retaliated, and passed personal liberty
bills, and other acts of a similar purport. Hatred
increased, and was intensified. It broke up the
unity of the churches, destroyed one great national
party, and disorganized for the time the other, and
at last organized and gave success to a purely sectional party organization. The people of the South,
influenced by the spirit of hate, and excited by the
struggle, believed that this success was the signal
for an attack upon their constitutional rights, and
the radicals of the North refused to do what was
indispensable to correct the apprehension, and the
result was war. Hatred aggravated and intensified
between neighbors finds cause or pretext for per-
'sonal conflict, and no people, under a free government can long dwell together with hatred rankling
'in their hearts, the one portion against the other,
without civil war, upon some misapprehension or
pretext.

The authors of the new policy are not only wrong
in their theory that slavery is the cause of the war,
and a destructive element in our political system,
but the policy they base on it is entirely antagonistic to the principles which must govern us if we
would restore the Union; and if successfully accomplished would furnish a fruitful cause of civil dissensions in the future.

This policy cannot be consummated without stamp-
ing the States, in which it is accomplished, with hu-

miliation. Their assertion is, that this right — the authority to hold slaves, is exercised by only a minority of the people of the States in rebellion, contrary to the interests, and even wishes of the majority, and that this forcible interference with slavery will be approved by the majority. In reply to this, it is sufficient to say that this majority can fairly be presumed to understand their own interests better than their philanthropic neighbors; and that if they desire, being in the majority, to be relieved of the system, they can easily effect it at the ballot-box. But further, and still more important, the right to hold slaves is a right, which although exercised only by a minority, attaches to the entire people of the States where it is permitted, and a forcible and illegal interference with it, is an insult to the dignity and character of the State, and will be resented by the whole people, independent of their personal interest in the privileges it grants, or even of their opinion of its utility, or of the expediency of continuing the right.

If the President or Congress, upon any pretence, should interfere with any right of the citizens of Massachusetts under the Constitution, even if that right were unimportant and of insignificant practical value, would not the act be resented by the whole people as an insult and usurpation? and could the people be ever appeased until reparation was made? In the suppression of the rebellion, the army may appropriate for its use, or destroy, as the necessities of the exigency shall require, any property of the enemy that may be reached. This is an acknowledged power incident to such a contest, and however much property of the people of the territory occupied by the army may be taken, in the proper exercise of this power, no cause of resentment will be occasioned which will survive the war. But if the Government shall, by force, annul a right which, under the Constitution, is to be perpetual except through the consent of the people, it will afford a constant cause of dissatisfaction and of discontent in the future. Slaves that are reached, or who shall come within our lines, whilst the war is being waged, may be freed; but the assertion that if, at the close of the war, any slaves are not thus liberated, the right of the master to hold them is annulled or can be annulled, without the consent of the people, through a proclamation or other act of the President, will never, in the present or in the future, be willingly acquiesced in by the people of the States possessing the right.

If peace could be restored, and the people of the States in rebellion be permitted to exercise all their rights under the Constitution excepting this one, could we look for a permanent peace in the future? Would not the act itself humiliate the State in which it should be exercised, and would not every man in the State feel the humiliation? Even if we could so far subjugate the people of the States in insurrection, as to seize and confiscate a considerable portion of their lands, and apportion them to our soldiers, and they should settle upon them and possess them peaceably, would they be exempt from this feeling? Would they not become identified with the interests of the section which was to be the home of themselves and their children, and within a brief period partake of and become imbued with all its feelings and prejudices? Would they not soon learn to resent the humiliation to which their section had been subjected, as strongly as those who were born upon its soil? Would not this new, and as it is claimed, stronger and more efficient portion of the population, afford to the section an increased strength in future struggles to wipe out the disgrace.

The theory of the new policy points inevitably toward disunion. Even if the authors of it could reach to the visionary result which they aim .to accomplish, it could be done only by planting the seeds of eternal discord. The consummation of their scheme would be the signal for other and more determined dissensions, and destructive of the future peace of the country. The President in adopting the new policy, repudiated the promises and the platform to which he pledged his administration in his inaugural message. The policy itself renders conciliation inadmissible, and under it, notwithstanding the favorable opportunities of the past few months, no overtures for adjustment have been made.

Lord Chatham, when measures of force alone had governed in the prosecution of the war against America for more that two years, said in the British Parliament, upon the proposition of an address to the throne upon the subject, "You cannot *conciliate* America by your present measures. You cannot *subdue* her by your present, or by any measures." And we say to the Administration, you cannot *conciliate* the South by your present measures, you cannot *subdue* her by your present, or by any measures, if you persistently refuse conciliation. But it is said, it does not comport with the dignity of the nation to proffer conciliation—that no accommodation should be attempted with rebels in arms. So thought the administration of Lord North, in the war of the Revolution. The war was prosecuted upon this policy for nearly three years, when Parliament interposed, passed conciliatory acts, under which commissioners were sent to America with full instructions and authority to treat with rebels in arms. The terms proposed were such as America would have originally complied with. But the proffer came too late. It came when, in the words of the historian Marshall, "All those affections which parts of the same empire should feel for each other, had been eradicated by a distressing war;

and the great body of the nation was determined, at every sacrifice, to maintain its independence." England was not humiliated by the offer. She was humbled only from the fact that she delayed it so long. Our administration may well seek instruction from this great lesson of history.

There is nothing plainer than that this struggle must result in the restoration of the Union through the consent, ultimately to be obtained, of the people of both sections, or in disunion. The first result cannot be attained by the sword alone. The grievances or apprehension that caused the war must be removed. By conciliation, influential men of the South must be won back to a love for the Union, and through their co-operation under such a policy the military power of the rebellion will be weakened, with a vigorous effort it may be overcome, and we may reasonably hope for a return of the masses to loyalty at no distant period. Any other policy must end in separation. Wild projects of subjugation may be attempted, and prosecuted under the excitements of the crisis, to the exhaustion of the people. They will not only end in disunion, if persisted in, but tend to prevent a permanent peace between the new governments that succeed. The hatred that will have culminated in the separation, will be handed down from generation to generation by both people, and constantly endanger their peace, on the slightest pretexts.

The people of the country should faithfully and
carefully examine these important subjects, and wisely determine what their highest duty to their country requires of them at the present crisis.  Above
all, let them not be mistaken in their judgment upon
the true criterion of loyalty and of patriotism.  The
stern and inexorable future alone will decide impar-
tially and correctly upon the events that are now
transpiring.  If the Union shall be restored, the
Constitution preserved in the future, the memory of
those who, amid perils, demanded and finally obtained the adoption of the policy which secured them,
will be blessed through all coming time; and if on
the other hand, through madness and fanaticism, the
colossal pillars of the noblest government the world
has ever known shall be pulled down, the Union dissolved and the government destroyed, the descendants of this great people, amid their execrations
against the authors of this terrible calamity, will remember with gratitude and admiration those men
who, amid the pitiless peltings of the storm, stood
true to the Constitution and the Union.  The Administration that persisted in the attempt to conquer
the rebellion in America by the sword alone, stands
to-day condemned before England and the world,
whilst Chatham and Burke and the other noble
statesmen who understood and defended the true
policy and interests of the nation against the passions of an excited majority, are known and believed

by all men to have been the truest and best friends
of their country. Let us, then, perform our duties
in the great future, calmly, discreetly and courageously. Let us, as faithful citizens, obey every lawful command of those who for the time administer
the affairs of the country, and on the other hand, let
us require of the Administration a faithful adherence to the Constitution, of the country, and the
adoption of such a policy as will bring us out of all
our perils, one people under the Union of our
fathers—a Union bound together with the ties of
kindred blood, mutual interests, and equality of
rights. This is the only Union that can be restored—it is the only Union worth restoring.

# SPEECH AT SALEM.*

The questions of our duty are connected with the colossal struggle in which the people of the country have been engaged for more than three years. These questions are to be met, and considered calmly, wisely, fully and courageously. In this hour of peril to our Union and our institutions, that man is not worthy the title of an American citizen who fails to utter his convictions and warnings, if he believes they may exert a salutary influence, however small, upon his fellow-citizens.

The questions proposed to every American citizen to-day are: What shall I do to preserve and perpetuate the great principles of civil liberty, upon which the governments of the States and of the Union are based? and how can I best act for the purpose of continuing the political relations which have existed between the people of the entire country, and conferred upon them such immeasurable benefits in the past? I state the issues in the order of

*Delivered before the Democratic Convention at Salem, April 21, 1864.

their importance. For, for one, I prefer to live in a country no larger than Massachusetts alone would constitute, with the blessings and privileges of the principles of self-government unimpaired, than dwell in a nation embracing the entire continent, over-shadowed and darkened by the black wings of a despotism.

The war on the part of the Government was commenced for the declared purpose of restoring the Union and the Constitution. It was believed that a majority of the people of the South desired the continuance of the Union, but were controlled by an excited and desperate minority who had possessed themselves of the reins of the State Governments, and the object of the people of the North was to suppress armed rebellion, and give to the real majority the supremacy in the seceded States. The result was to be accomplished not by the overthrow, but through the instrumentality of the principles of self-government. The people of the North, uninfluenced by the terrible passions which the war has since excited, then believed that the Union could and should be restored only through the consent of the majority of the people of the several States. I believe now that the only way the Union can be restored or any Union reconstructed is through the voluntary cooperation of the people of the different sections of the country. There can be no other union upon republican principles. There may be theoretically a unity extorted and sustained by force, such as now exists and is maintained between Russia and Poland and between Austria and Hungary—a despotic power and a people acquiescing only through military coercion which it is powerless to resist—such a unity will dissolve the moment the armed hand is removed, a unity which, if it could be compelled in this country, would be scarcely less oppressive to the conquering than to the conquered section. It is true in our own experience, that an attempt to subjugate one portion of the people is, and can only be prosecuted by the exercise of despotic power. The constitutional liberties of the people are now suspended, their rights under the laws denied, and the principles of self-government subordinated to the will of the Federal Executive. The President claims that it is necessary for him to assume these powers in the prosecution of the war, and that he is authorized to exercise them from military necessity. If this claim is a correct one the despotic and anti-republican character of the acts is not changed. No one will deny that if the present exigencies demand and justify such exercise . of power, the same necessity will require a continuance of their use so long as the exigencies continue; and that if these exigencies shall be perpetual in duration, then that we must have a perpetual despotism, strengthening and increasing as all power does in its exercise. It is true that a large portion

of the people have not personally felt the inflictions
of the despotism which exists. Power is invariably obsequious, and conceals its serpent head under
specious pretexts, until it is securely planted on its
throne; but from the moment it gets seated and confirmed, it makes no distinctions among the people in
its exactions. Under institutions like ours, it avails
itself of the spirit and passion of party in a time of
great popular excitement, to cover the inception and
progress of its aggressions upon the liberties of the
people, but when it once obtains a sure foothold it
makes no distinction of party. Confirmed despotism sympathizes with, and receives sympathy, from no
party of the people. It bestows its favors upon a
few sycophants, and the people of all parties are
equally its subjects.

If subjugation of the South, should be practically
accomplished, there will continue the same necessity for the application of force that now exists.
If the entire scheme of the Administration could
be consummated, and we obtain military possession
of every State which has seceded, and find one-tenth
of the people who can be induced to take the prescribed oath, and elect State and Federal officers,
will it not require as large a force at least as is now
employed, to protect the Government of one-tenth
against the power of the other nine-tenths? So
long as the policy of subjugation is persisted in, we
must live under arbitrary military power, and a na-

tional unity, based upon its successful issue, can be sustained only by a continued exercise of the same power.

There can be no union of the people of the different sections of the country with our republican institutions preserved, without it is based ultimately upon the free exercise of the right of self-government in the people of the several States. The declared policy of the Administration is now subjugation. It has announced its determination to prosecute the war not for the purpose of effecting a result which will permit the people of the South to exercise the rights of self-government, but for the purpose of compelling the adoption of such constitutions and laws in the several States of that section as the dominant party of the other section of the country, or its representatives, shall prescribe. These results, the experience of the world and human reason teach can be accomplished only through a thorough subjugation and keeping in subjection, or in the extermination of the people of the South. The principles of self-government are refused the people of the Southern States, and in their place is attempted to be substituted a power in one-tenth who have subscribed to the oath under the so-called amnesty proclamation, to rule over the other nine-tenths, and that oath taken in most instances through the influence of military power, for without this influence there is not a State in the South in which

one-tenth of the people can be found to acquiesce
in the policy and requirements of the Federal Executive.

This policy of the Administration is sustained in
full by the Republican party of the North, and so
strong are the passions and animosities excited in
the war, that if the people now resisting the authority of the General Government should offer to lay
down their arms, subject to all the penalties prescribed by the Constitution, upon the sole condition
of a restoration or reconstruction of the Union,
based upon the rights and privileges established by
that great charter of our liberties, it is plain that
the Republican party would refuse the offer. The
war has been and is prosecuted under this declared
policy of the Administration. More than three
years of terrible blood-shed show the desperate
character of the undertaking. Without considering
the enormous sacrifice in blood and treasure which
must be made in the further prosecution of the war
under such a policy, or the uncertainty, at least, of
its successful issue, I believe that if the subjugation
and practical extermination of the people of the
South could be accomplished, it could be effected
only through such an exercise of power as the God
of Heaven would frown upon, and that the day of
its consummation would mark the saddest era in the
history of the people of the North. From that day
they would live under a Government not depending

upon the consent of the governed. On the shaft that would commemorate the consummation of the policy of subjugation, and the emancipation by it of four millions of negroes, would be inscribed the epitaph of the liberties of thirty millions of people—who voluntarily acquiesced in the destruction of a political system, under which they and their fathers had enjoyed greater freedom, prosperity, and happiness than was ever before vouchsafed to any other people under the light of the sun.

The idea of a compelled Union is preposterous. The Union under which we have lived was not created by compulsion, it cannot be continued by compulsion. Whilst a majority at the South really favored the Union, there was hope of restoring it by giving them the supremacy in the seceded States; but now that every man of influence at the South has been driven from our cause, there can be no possibility of reunion, without their being first conciliated. The policy of the Administration is not intended for conciliation. It is with every day confirming hatred against the Government, and rendering a restoration of the Union more impossible, and it is now a most momentous question whether, under any change of policy or administration, reconciliation can be effected. If the people of the country would revert to the principles on which the Union was established, and, instead of hatred, would cherish a love and respect for each other, we could hope for a reunion, not otherwise. Constitutions, laws forced consent, do not make a Union, any more than the marriage ceremony can unite hearts which have no sympathy with each other. The Constitution did not create the Union. It existed in the hearts of the people of the different States, and the Constitution was its open recognition and the golden bond which encircled it. The Constitution would not have been worth the parchment on which it was written, without the fact of a pre-existing Union, and it has no power in itself to compel a Union in the future, if the fraternal spirit which created the Union shall have been destroyed.

If, in the providence of God, the people of this generation are doomed to witness the destruction of the American Union, the spectacle will bring no sorrow to the hearts of those who for long years have prayed for such a consummation, and but little of regret to those who, intoxicated with the excitements of the time, have anticipated the event, and thanked God that the Union was gone, never to return.

The only real, sincere, heartfelt mourners at the grave of the Union will be the conservative men of the country. They have in the past enjoyed its priceless blessings with gratitude, and performed all its requirements with cheerfulness. They have stood by it in good report and in evil report—in prosperity and in adversity—in peace and in war;

and they will stand by it now, so long as there is a ray of hope that this great people may be again reconciled.

# SPEECH IN FANEUIL HALL.*

Historians relate that after a long and cruel war between the Romans and the Samnites, the Samnite people were exhausted and asked for terms which the Romans refused to give. In this emergency the Samnite General, by an adroit movement, drew the whole Roman army into a dark defile. The Roman General when too late, suspected a snare, and attempted to retrace his steps, when he found the entrance and the craggy heights on either side of the defile, commanded by the Samnite troops. The entire Roman army was completely in the power of the Samnites. Caius Pontius, the Samnite General, deliberated upon the course he should pursue, and sent for advice to his aged father, the wise Herennius. The old man came to the camp and pronounced this oracle: "kill them all, or send them all back with honor; destroy your enemies, or make friends of them." Historians further relate that the Samnite General refused to follow either of these counsels, and that he required the Roman army to pass under the yoke

---

*Delivered in Faneuil Hall at the Convention for election of Delegates to the Philadelphia Convention, August 8, 1866.

thereby inflicting upon it the greatest humiliation; and history further records the details of a war of more than thirty years duration between the Romans and the Samnites, as the result of that humiliation, unprecedented in the cruelty with which it was prosecuted, and in the amount of blood that was shed.

These great facts of history, are full of instruction and warning to the American people. For the future peace of the country, there has been but one of two policies to be pursued since the close of the war. Either to make a wilderness of the fertile acres of the South, and to so far crush all hope of liberty in the future, that her population could be held impassive in our iron grasp, or to restore to her people the rights of American citizens, treat them with magnanimity and honor, encourage their hopes, and stimulate their industry.

These alternatives were presented to the Generals who commanded our armies at the close of the war. They spurned the first, as unworthy the American name and character, and on the battle-field, amid the plaudits of their gallant troops, offered to the brave men who had surrendered, the fullest amnesty, and required of them only that they should peaceably return to their homes and obey the laws. This conduct was met with a hearty approval from the great mass of the American people. The partisan leaders alone objected to it. They thought they saw in the spirit of the act, the subsidence of the partisan passion and sectional hatred, to which they owed their prominence and positions.

But the will of the people was too strong and unmistakable, to be openly resisted. It was not deemed prudent by the radical leaders, to demand that the South be blotted out of the Union, and her people held as slaves to the North. They pretended to acquiesce in the popular will, but claimed that the interests of the country required that the Southern States should be restored to the Union, only after a period of probation; they asked only for delay. They proposed only that the white people of the South should be held for an indefinite time by military power; and, as it was necessary for their party success that they should secure the votes of these States whilst thus held, they devised a plan of organizing governments, to be controlled, through the instrumentality of enfranchised negroes, protected by the military, and directed by the officers of the Freedmen's Bureau.

These partisan leaders observed a worse than punic faith, not only with the people of the South, but with the people of the North. They refused to be governed by the principles which the people of the South understood by the terms of the capitulation of their armies, were to be applied to that section, and through plausible pretexts they thwarted the will of the people of the North. Their object was

political power. They well knew that if the white
people of the South should be allowed their rights
under the Constitution, they would act politically
with the Conservative party of the North, which
would give to it the numerical majority in the
country. Their object was to prevent this. These
men who have prated so loudly within the past few
years of the divine rights of the majority, and of
the duty of the minority to acquiesce in its will, have
determined, as the only means of perpetuating their
own power, to make by force the majority subser-
vient to the minority. It requires no argument
from me to show that this is entirely subversive of
republican principles. If it was claimed by these
leaders that there should be further protection to
minorities, it would be concurred in by the conserva-
tives as the Constitution was framed for the
purpose of protecting minority interests; and if the
protection it gives is insufficient, it is legitimate to
make an amendment to give further protection.
New England claimed in 1814, that the Constitution gave inadequate protection to the interests of
minorities, and the South has made the same claim
since.  It is one thing however to give to the minority power to protect itself, through checks upon the
action  of the majority, and quite another thing to
empower the minority to legislate against the will
of the majority.

But aside from the anti-republican principles of

the policy of the radical leaders, what must be the practical effect of that policy upon the interests of the Union. They admit that the Constitutional rights of the people of the South, must at some future period be restored to them; that it is only a question of time. Is it then expedient that there shall be any delay in restoring these rights? Can the people of the South be trusted after five or ten years of abuse out of the Union, better than they can be if permitted the rights of American citizens to-day. Will unkind and unchristian treatment of years cause the people of the South to love us better than they do now? Cruel punishments, and deprivations never yet brought love and respect. Every one knows that hatred and animosities are fearfully increased with every day of a postponed Union. Every one knows that the sentiment of the people of the South in favor of a restored Union is not nearly so strong as it was a year ago. It will be weakened with every act under the present policy. If the sole object of the radical leaders in Congress was to render a restored Union impossible, they could have devised no more effective method to accomplish it than the one they are now pursuing.

The president of the United States, mindful of his high duties, and of his oath to preserve, protect and defend the Constitution of the United States, has fearlessly and most ably opposed the entire policy of the Radical Congress. He has stood alone and

employed all the powers that were vested in him by
virtue of his high office, to resist its attempted usurpations, looking anxiously forward to the time when
the Constitution loving people of the country would
rally to his support.    The Convention to be held at
Philadelphia is called for the purpose of expressing
the will of the people.    I believe if the members of
that Convention shall act with wisdom and patriotism, they will render important service in the salvation of the country, and that at no distant day
the people of every State will be represented in the
Congress of the Union, and such protection given to
all the great and important interests of the country
as to prevent any jealousies or conflicts in the future, and that then again, the whole American people will proclaim in the words of the defender of the
Constitution: "Liberty and Union, now and forever,
one and inseparable."

# SPEECH AT MANCHESTER.*

It is now nearly three years since the people of
the North rejoiced at the termination of the war, accomplished with the complete triumph of their armies, and looked hopefully forward to the immediate
practical reunion of the disrupted sections of the
country under the system, and in accordance with
the principles, which had united them in the prosperous and happy past. They expected that, this result accomplished, the great productive interests of
the South would be revived, and many believed they
would be revived under more favorable auspices than
before the war, and that consequent upon the renewed prosperity of that great section, the commercial, manufacturing and other great interests of the
country would be reinvigorated, and gradually, but
speedily restored to the condition of permanent
prosperity which they enjoyed at the commencement
of the struggle. It was then universally hoped and
believed, that with the strength and confidence this
expected state of affairs would give, with rigid

*Delivered at Manchester, N. H., January 22, 1868.

economy in the administration of the government, and the vast reduction of expenditures incident to a return to the rule of the constitution, the country could bear the burden the war had entailed upon it, and that the business of the country could be brought back to the constitutional currency, which was deemed indispensable to its healthful and prosperous condition.

But now after such a long interval of time, instead of rejoicing in the realization of their reasonable hopes, the people of the North are oppressed with feelings of uncertainty and anxiety in regard to all their important interests, greater than at any period in their past history. In the nearly three years that have thus elapsed, the political relations of the South to the Union have not been restored, its productive interests have not been revived, and largely as a consequence, the commercial, manufacturing and other industrial interests of the North have languished, and are now in a condition which causes disquietude and alarm.

The agricultural sections of the North feel sensibly the great diminution in the demands of the South for their cereals; the manufacturing sections feel no less sensibly the substantial loss of so great a market for their fabrics, and the largely decreased production of the great staple which is the basis of their manufacture, and its consequent enhanced price, render their future prosperity doubtful. Our commerce, which depends largely on the export of the great product of the South, which before the war was of more value than all our other exports combined, feels most sensibly the loss, as its present depressed condition and the balances of our merchants abroad abundantly prove.

With this depression of the great business interests of the country, the extraordinary expenses of policies outside the Constitution have been and are continued, and increased; and reckless extravagance instead of rigid economy, is practiced in all the expenditures of the General Government.

Why are these things so? Are the people of the South unwilling to resume their position under the Constitution, and does there exist a necessity for the continuance of vast extra-constitutional expenditures for the purpose of protecting the government, which is the only ground on which the exercise of powers not enumerated in the Constitution has been claimed?

The South, from the day of the surrender of its armies, has been absolutely powerless of aggressive action. This every man at the North knows and believes. In no quarter of that vast section, in the time that has elapsed since the close of the war, has there been manifested any desire or intention to renew the struggle. From the hour the people of the South abandoned their hope of independence, they have earnestly sought and pleaded for a full resto-

ration of the Union under the Constitution. Without a murmur they yielded up their immense property in slaves, and passed ordinances for the repudiation
of the debts of their communities contracted in the
struggle, for the purpose of effecting the restoration
of their relations to the Union, and as an earnest
of their good faith in the future. Everything that
a great, civilized and Christian people could do, consistent with honor and the future welfare of their
communities, the people of the South have done, to
restore the Union, and to re-assert the rule of the
Constitution throughout their section.

But how has this conduct on the part of the people
of the South been met by the people of the North?
The Congress of the United States which represents
them, and is so united in its action as to control all
the powers of legislation, has persistently refused
all overtures made by the South, has refused to acknowledge their constitutional local governments,
has refused to receive the States of that section back
into the Union, and to acknowledge, or allow a seat
in its body, to their Representatives duly elected in
accordance with the provisions of the Constitution
of the United States, and has held, and is now holding, the States of that entire section by military
power. This is not all. It not only has held, and
now holds, these States under military rule, with
armed soldiery quartered in every District, but
whilst thus holding them, has disfranchised the better

and more influential portion of the white population, given the ballot to the emancipated negroes, who, in many States constituted a majority of the population, stationed partisan officers at the polls, and have gone through with the wicked mockery of the form of holding elections.  As if it were not a sufficient oppression and humiliation of the people of the South, to refuse them a voice in the General Government, and to supersede their constitutional local governments by military rule, Congress is practising upon them the refinement of cruelty and insult, by securing the pretended formal consent of their communities to its acts and partisan policies, enforced by the bayonet, and expressed through the ballots of negroes and far more degraded white men, against the intelligence of the better portion of the white population which is forbidden any participation in the elections.  A more cruel, wicked, diabolical treatment was never before attempted by a civilized government on a christian people.  Prussia holds Poland; Austria, Hungary; England, Ireland, by force of military power, but neither of these governments, in the face of the civilized world, has ever attempted or dared attempt, through such a degrading policy to extort a consent to oppression, from the victims of their tyranny.

The purpose of Congress in the adoption of these extra constitutional measures must be, either to permanently hold these States by military power, or

eventually to commit the destinies of one of the
most important of the great sections of the country
into the hands of the emancipated negroes who will
constitute in most of the States a majority of the
voting population. Congress has declared the latter to be its purpose. Better, far better, for the
interests of the South; better, far better for republican institutions in the future, that that fair section
be forever held in the most relentless military grasp.
Peace and order might then for a portion of the
time at least be maintained, and an opportunity giv-
en for a partial development of the great interests
of that section; and the policy of the government,
while it would bring Republican principles into contempt, would not necessarily work their ruin.

But entrust the great interests of that section to
the control of negroes, inferior in natural capacity,
degraded as the authors of the policy declare by
centuries of oppression uneducated, without any conception of the proprieties and obligations of civilized
life, with no knowledge, or traditions even, of our
form of government, and if not relieved through
revolution, a howling wilderness will be made of the
fertile acres of the South, and not only reproach, but
destruction, brought to Republican institutions in ten
States of the American Union. But this result I
believe a wise and just God will never permit to be
accomplished. If persisted in, it will in time bring
revolution and a war of races, in which the weaker

will go down.

Five millions of American people nurtured in the spirit of American liberty, and educated in the prin- ciples of the American system of government, may be overpowered, may be oppressed and down-trodden for the time, but can never be made slaves. Inhab- iting a territory larger than the territories of Great Britain, France, Austria and Prussia combined, with a climate unsurpassed, and productions more varied abundant and rich than any territory of similar ex- tent on the face of the globe, they are not to be ex- terminated or enslaved, or their lands roamed over by mongrels and negroes.

But whatever may be the effect of the policy of Congress upon the liberties of the people of the South, or on the future of Republican principles, so long as it is persisted in, all the great and impor- tant interests of that section will be uncared for, and all energy and enterprise paralyzed. Good gov- ernment is indispensable for the prosperity of any community. Held under military rule, or governed by negroes, with the entire system of labor disor- ganized, how can the country hope for any restora- tion of the interests of the South, or expect any- thing but further deterioration with the progress of time ? What capitalist from abroad will seek invest- ment in a province under negro rule, or what hardy laborer of the Caucasian race can be induced to make there a home for himself and his family ? Does even any enterprising friend of the policy from the North, notwithstanding the great cheapness of the lands, venture to go to the South and live under the policy he has assisted to prescribe for that section?

But what must be the effect of this conduct toward the South upon the public securities of the country? To say nothing of the loss of revenue it must occasion from the unproductiveness of an entire section, is there nothing to be apprehended from it in the future, from the accession to our voting population of four millions of negroes, not one of whom owns a dollar in the bonds of the government? Ignorant though they are, the instincts of self-interest will not be found wanting.

They will be found voting in a body for the most extravagant expenditures, as it is the radical boast they did several months since in one of the most important cities of the South, where they with unanimity, voted the credit of the municipality in which they voted, for $2,000,000, in a single day; the credit really of the white population which was forbidden to vote. The same class will, as unanimously and more enthusiastically in the future, vote for the repudiation of all obligations which detract from the income of their labor. But more directly and inevitably does this extra-constitutional policy toward the South tend to, aye accomplish, repudiation, from the necessary absorption of the revenues of the country which it requires. Never, before the war, did the annual expenses of the government exceed about $75, 000, 000. The last year, the expenses of the government, exclusive of interest and pensions, amounted to about $200, 000, 000. The Radical leaders openly avow that the expenses of the government must be necessarily large in the future, and it is undeniable, if their policy is to be continued. They must be constantly increasing. The difference between the amount of the anual expenses before and since the war, or rather the expenses of the extra-constitutional policy is sufficient to pay nearly, if not quite, five per cent. on the entire present amount of the indebtedness of the United States.

The danger of repudiation in the future is far greater from the inability of the country to furnish sufficient revenue for the payment of the debt, than from any formal action of the people to rid themselves of their burdens. The business of the country is now taxed to the fullest extent.—Any increase would depress business without augmenting the revenue, yet it is evident that if we should effect a return to specie payments, the revenues would be insufficient to defray the probable expenses of the General Government under the present policy, and the interest on its indebtedness. If this is true, then either the expenses of the Government must be reduced, or we shall be unable to meet the demands of our public creditors upon such a consum-

mation. It should be remembered that the actual
expenses of the government constitute the first claim
upon the treasury. They must be first paid before
any appropriations can be made for the public debt.
Therefore the solution of the question of our ability
to meet our indebtedness in the future depends
largely, if not entirely, upon the determination of
the question of what the annual expenditures of the
General Government are to be. It is useless to
speculate upon the amount that can be applied an-
nually to the principal or interest of our bonds,
until it is determined with approximate correctness
at least, what the prior claims on the treasury—the
annual expenses of the government are to be.

The most important enquiry then as affecting the
value of our public securities is, are the expenses
of the General Government to be increased, or even
to be continued as at present, or are they to be reduced? Are we to perpetuate the policy of extra-
constitutional appropriations for an army of over
50, 000 men, for officers and men of the Freedmen's
Bureau throughout the South, and for all other appli-
ances necessary to carry out and maintain the entire
radical scheme in that section. The paramount question for those interested in our public
securities to-day, is that of retrenchment, by returning to the rule of the constitution, saving to the
country an annual expenditure nearly sufficient to
pay our entire interest, and thereby putting the

people of the Southern States in a position to contribute something to the treasury of the country.

The perfidy of this entire Radical scheme for the
oppression of the white people of the South at an
annual expense of scarcely less than $100,000,000
to the tax-payers of the country, is paralleled only
by the mendacity with which its authors in Congress
attempt to justify their acts with the people of the
North. They assert that their policy is demanded
to carry into effect the purposes for which the war
was waged. No such purpose was ever declared
before, or during, the war. Congress declared by
solemn resolve in the commencement of the struggle,
that the war was waged not in any spirit of oppression, nor for conquest or subjugation, but to defend
and maintain the supremacy of the Constitution, and
preserve the Union, with all the dignity, equality and
rights of the several States, unimpaired. This
pledge was repeated by the Executive and Legislative departments during the war. No proclamation
was ever made to the army that they were to fight
for the establishment of negro suffrage, and it is
plain that if it had been, no armies would have volunteered for the purpose, and the war would not
have been conducted under the auspicies which in-
sured the final triumph of our arms. No such purpose was understood by the army, or by the masses
of the people at the North. If such a purpose was
contemplated by the radical Congressional leaders,

it would tend strongly to justify the charge that has been made, that the war was desired by them only for partisan purposes, and that they entered upon and conducted it as they would a political campaign, for power and place—in other words that they regarded the great civil war, and the slaughter of hundreds of thousands of brave men, only as a means for the maintenance and perpetuity of the political organization of which they were the leaders.

Professing to be honest champions of universal suffrage, these same Congressional leaders claim that every negro, without any discrimination regarding his capacity or intelligence, has a natural and inalienable right to exercise the elective franchise, and they denounce the masses at the North, acting under the old Democratic banner who deny this postulate, as illiberal, and opposed to the progressive spirit of republican principles. Let us apply to these high-sounding pretensions the test of experience in our past history. From the first settlement of the country to the present time, great, fundamental, antagonistic tendencies upon questions underlying those of suffrage, have characterized the respective political parties. The one party comprising the wealth of the country and the masses it could control, has naturally and strongly favored and tended to strengthen the power and prerogatives of government. Its tendency has been towards a government of the few. The other party comprising the bold, intellectual strength and statesmanship of the country, and sustained by the independent laboring masses, has tended toward a government of the whole people. The one largely representing capital, has been distrustful of the numerical strength of the masses representing labor. The other, with a respect for capital, and a regard for its safety, has been distrustful of *its* political influence, and has reposed confidence in the masses representing ¡labor, with the conviction that labor would in the natural order of things, in every community, work in harmony with capital, and that where their proper relations were not disturbed, its democratic tendency would only serve as a salutary check and offset to the aristocratic tendencies of wealth. At the period of the commencement of the Revolution, the tendency in one party of the people was toward a continuance of our relations with Great Britain, under the belief that its power was indispensable for the order and well being of the Country. The tendency in the other party was toward independence and a government of the whole people. The leaders of both parties undoubtedly acted upon their convictions regarding the public good. But the popular party succeeded, and large numbers of their opponents expatriated themselves, under the belief that there would be no safety for persons or property under a government of the whole people. After the close of the Revo-

lution, the contest was renewed under issues growing out of the altered circumstances of the country.
Under the leadership of Thomas Jefferson, the
party of Democratic tendencies prevailed, and governed in the affairs of the country, almost without
intermission until 1861. The fundamental principles of that party are historic, and have been fully
exemplified through administrations covering half a
century. The Democratic party has ever been
based on an unswerving faith in the capacity and
virtue in the people for self-government. During
this entire period it never faltered in its trust in
the people. It freely and cordially welcomed to all
the rights of citizenship, the hardy sons of Europe
who sought in this country a home for themselves
and their descendants. This liberal policy contributed largely to swell the tide of immigration, and to
it, large, influential, and well governed States of the
Union are indebted for their present positions and
prosperity. These principles, and this policy of the
Democracy were constantly and vehemently assailed
by the opponents of the party, as tending too largely to strengthen and increase the democratic element in the government.

The leaders of the party of universal negro suffrage of to-day, excepting those who deserted the
Democratic party and its principles, have been in
the past the most bitter opponents of these principles and this policy of the Democracy. They have

doubted the virtue and wisdom in the masses of the people for self-government, and spent their lives in endeavoring to hedge in and restrict the exercise of the elective franchise by the laboring classes. The leaders of universal negro suffrage in New England to-day, were but a few years since the leaders in the so-called American, or Knownothing movement, which culminated in the Republican party. Under their leadership State Constitutions even, were amended so as to prohibit those of foreign birth from voting, unless they possessed prescribed educational qualifications.

There is little in the antecedents of the Radical leaders to impart confidence in their professions of regard for the laboring masses in connection with their policy of universal negro suffrage. They certainly have manifested no change of principle in their conduct toward the masses at the North, and there is much to show that in their policy toward the South they are actuated less by a regard for the negro than by a hatred of the white people of that section. Indeed, their entire action upon negro suffrage is only consistent with an intention of availing themselves of the liberal and popular democratic idea on suffrage, and of pushing it to a ruinous extreme, to bring into disrepute, and overwhelm, suffrage itself at the South.

In the natural and undisturbed order of things, an inferior and degraded race would be largely influenced and controlled by the wealth of their respective communities; and if to the people of each Southern State had been left the management of their own affairs, the relations of capital and labor would perhaps have been adjusted so that little danger of collision between the different classes would have been apprehended. But the special policy of the Radical leaders has been to divorce and estrange the masses of the negroes from the white population representing the capital of their respective communities, through the forcible interposition of alien agents supported by the military authorities, so that all equilibrium of interests has been destroyed, and to the negroes, being numerically the stronger party, have been given practically the control in all matters of legislation.

I believe that the people of the country are beginning to see through these mischievous pretensions of the radical leaders, and to understand that the Democratic party now, as in the past, is the party of rational liberality, not only on direct questions of suffrage, but upon all questions which affect the laboring masses of the country. Upon questions of suffrage, taxation, payment of the bonds, the banks and the currency, the radical party is largely supported by, and in return supports the demands of capital, with but little regard for the interests or welfare of the laboring classes. The Democratic party now, and in the future, whilst it will concede to capital all it can legitimately demand, will jealously and fearlessly guard the rights and claims of labor, against its power and encroachments. At no time in the history of the country have democratic principles been so essential for the interests and happiness of the masses of the people as now.

I have thus attempted, briefly, to point to the mischievous and and disorganizing policy of the radical leaders, and to expose some of the pretexts under which they have attempted to justify their acts with the people of the North. Language is inadequate to express the misery and demoralization which the perpetuation of their rule must inevitably bring to the people of the country.

History records no such wonderful achievements as have been witnessed in the experience of this country in the past. For nearly a century, all the vast and varied interests of this great Continent, excepting the narrow belt on its northern border, have been made to fully harmonize under a wise and beneficent system of reciprocity, maintained and protected by the checks and balances provided in the Constitution of the Union. Originally, in all essential characteristics two nationalities, expanding with the developements of the West and Pacific slope, into four, we have maintained a Union politically, and a complete co-operation of resources materially. In our later history the rich Pacific section has poured into our coffers wealth, from its mines of the precious metals, and from its agriculture. The great West has supplied largely to the South, from its fertile prairies, cereals for the support of its population engaged in a more profitable culture, and has found a generous market at the East. The Eastern and Middle sections, from their mines and manufactories have helped largely to supply to the people of the other sections their necessary utensils and fabrics, and from their manufacturing communities to support a large agricultural population at home. The South, from profitable crops of its important staple, has not only fed all the manufactories of fabrics at the East, but has been our great representative of wealth abroad. All these immense and diverse interests, under our wonderful Constitutional system, have been made to fully co-operate, and together they have created the prosperity which characterized the Country at the commencement of the war. The great interests of neither of these Sections can be prostrated without the whole Country feeling the shock.

The productions of no Section have contributed more in the past, nor are so essential to-day, for the prosperity of the whole Country, and especially for that portion of it in which our lot is cast, as those of the South. The cotton of that section, if not King, has been the source of immense wealth to the Country, and without it, New England prosperity is a thing of the past. If the extensive cultivation of this staple is not revived, and that speedily, the manufacture of cotton fabrics in this section must be abandoned. Already Europe, impelled by necessity, has caused its extensive cultivation in India and Egypt, and although the plant there grown is not of so good an average fibre as that of the South, yet from it, with improved machinery, the best of fabrics are woven. With, or without protective duties, the manufacturers of England can compete successfully with the manufacturers of the United States, not only abroad, but in our own markets. Cheap cotton at the South is the only salvation to our manufacturers. If that never comes, our factories will be closed, our manufacturing population will be compelled elsewhere, and in other occupations, to seek a living, our commerce will continue to be depressed, and our agricultural population deprived of a home market for their produce, will eke a scanty subsistence from their labor in the fields.

But these calamities may be averted. With statesmanship in the councils of the General Government—with a united will on the part of the people to make all mere partisan considerations subordinate to a fixed determination of fully restoring the Union, and of repairing what the ravages of war have pros. trated—much, perhaps all, may yet be saved. Bring back the country to the rule of the Constitution— reduce the expenditures of the government to appropriations only for constitutional purposes—require rigid economy and the simplicity of the early days of the republic in the management of the affairs of the General Government—disband the army that is now quartered on the South—abolish the Freedmen's Bureau and other expensive and unnecessary Departments which are supported on the substance of the people—reduce the expenses of collecting the revenues—dismiss the force of supernumerary office-holders, more voracious and destructive than were the locusts of Egypt—reinvest the States with the rights that have been torn from them—reassert local self-government—trust the people—and confidence will be restored; enterprise and energy will awaken at the South, business will revive, and all the great interests of the country receive an immense and lasting impulse.

But, Mr. President, I should do injustice to my feelings if I should close without turning from a discussion of the material and political affairs of the country, to express the sympathy I feel for the oppressed and down-trodden white population of the Southern section of our common country, in this hour of their terrible trial. My heart bleeds tonight for the millions of our own flesh and blood, united to us by kindred ties and the recollections and deeds of a glorious past—brave men, defenceless women and children, suffering a slavery at the hands of our own people, which, if perpetuated, will be worse to them than death. May a wise and good Providence give strength to the friends of the Constitution and the Union at the North, to hurl from their seats the authors of these oppressions, and to place in the councils of the country, men of humanity, men with a patriotism which looks beyond their own immediate neighborhoods, who will raise the people of the South from their present condition, and place them on the platform of equality to which they are entitled by nature and the Constitution of the Country—with the hope that from the gratitude of the saved and the generous sentiment of the saviors, there may grow up a new Union of American communities—a Union in the hearts of the people of all the sections, which shall bind them together with stronger and more enduring ties than the Union of the past.

# THE UNITED STATES CONSCRIPTION ACT*

There has been no act of the Federal Government during the present war, more important in its principles, or which more directly affects our institutions and the liberties of the people, for the present and the future, than the Conscription act, so called, of the last session of Congress.

The act asserts an authority in the United States Government to require the military service of every able-bodied man of the country, in the national force, through compulsion, for such period of service, upon such conditions, and under such organizations, as Congress may from time to time determine.

It is the first time in the history of the country that such an authority has been asserted by the Federal Government. It is an assertion which personally and most deeply interests every man in the country, capable of bearing arms. It is a power which, if sanctioned and exercised, reaches to, and must effect a material change in the principles upon which our free institutions and system of govern-

*Published in the Boston Courier, August 20, 1863.

ment have been thus far conducted.

It is an assertion which demands the most careful and critical consideration, to the end, that if it shall be found to be in consonance with the spirit of the Constitution, and the principles of civil liberty which that instrument was designed to protect, this onerous act, based upon it, may receive the approval and concurrence of the whole people, which is indispensable for its successful execution; and that if, on the other hand, it shall be proved to be in violation of the intentions of the people when they adopted the Constitution, and to be an unjustifiable departure from essential fundamental principles of our government, the act may be declared void by the judicial tribunals, or repealed by the body which passed it.

If there is authority for the act it is contained in the Constitution of the United States: The Constitution provides upon the subject, that Congress "Shall have power to declare war—to raise and support armies—but no appropriation of money to that use shall be for a longer time than two years—to provide for calling forth the militia to execute the laws of the Union, suppress insurrections and repel invasions—to provide for organizing, arming and disciplining the militia, and for governing such part of them as may be employed in the service of the United States, reserving to the States respectively, the appointment of the officers, and the authority of training the militia according to the discipline prescribed by Congress," and further that "The President shall be Commander-in-Chief of the *army* and navy of the *United States* and of the *Militia of the several States* when called into the service of the *United States*."

In the Amendments it is provided that "A well regulated militia being necessary to the security of a free State, the right of the people to keep and bear arms shall not be infringed."

A proper interpretation of these provisions will define the limit of the authority of the United States over the persons of the citizens, for military purposes.

In the amendments to the Constitution it is provided, that, "The powers not delegated to the United States by the Constitution, nor prohibited by it to the States, are reserved to the States respectively, or to the people."

At the time of the adoption of the Constitution, all powers of sovereignty and legislation resided in the several States and in the people. All the powers given to the United States by the Constitution were taken, carved, out of these powers of the States and the people. The rules of construction of the powers of the United States and of the States and the people are therefore not indentical.

The powers thus carved out are limited by the express words of the grant, and are not to be extended or determined in case of doubt, as against the powers of the States and the people, by process of analogy, or by implication. What is not clearly given is reserved.

What power, then, for obtaining men for military service is given to the United States by the Constitution?

1st. Exclusive authority to raise and maintain armies, restricted by the limitation of appropriations to its use to the term of two years, and by the provisions relating to the militia.

2d. Authority to require the aid of the militia of the States, to execute the laws of the Union, suppress insurrections and repel invasions, but for no other purposes, and for terms of service limited by the exigency on which they are called.

The Constitution does not define the terms "armies," and "militia," or the mode through which either force is to be raised, for the reason that both terms, and the mode of obtaining the respective forces, were perfectly well understood by the people at the time of its adoption.

The army was a force established in Great Britain before the settlement of the colonies. Upon the decadence of the feudal system, the policy of employing a regular and permanent national force, or standing army, was initiated.

This force was composed of men obtained, not by virtue of their obligations of allegiance to their sov-

ereign, but by contract; and contracts to serve in
this force were made, not only with those who owed
allegiance, but with aliens.  It was a hired, or as it
was sometimes styled, mercenary force, as it was
composed of men who voluntarily enlisted for the
pay they were to receive.

This system has been continued in Great Britain
to the present time without change, and although
the Government has been involved in wars of the
greatest magnitude, which threatened the integrity
of the empire, yet it never claimed an authority to
obtain men for this force by compulsion.

The Colonies adopted the same force, which was
continued by the States, during the Revolutionary
War.  The army, or regular army, during all the
trying emergencies of that great struggle, was raised
invariably by voluntary enlistments, by contract
between the States and those who were willing to
serve.

Early in the history of the Coloties another independent force was established, known as the Militia.
Like the army, it had its origin in the Mother Country.  It had existed in that country for a long period,
and in the 17th century was, by Statute, defined
and systematized.                                    .

"The general scheme" of which system, according
to Blackstone, "is to discipline a certain number of
the inhabitants of every county, chosen by lot for
*three* years, and officered by the Lord Lieutenant,

the Deputy Lieutenants, and other principal land holders, under a commission from the crown. They are not compellable to march out of their counties, unless in case of invasion or actual rebellion within the realm ( or any of its dominions or territories, ) nor in any case compellable to march out of the kingdom. They are to be exercised at stated times and their discipline in general, is liberal and easy; but when drawn out into actual service, they are subject to the rigors of martial law, as necessary to keep them in order. This is the constitutional security which our laws have provided for the public peace, and for protecting the realm against foreign or domestic violence."

Under the system thus established in this country the whole body of the people of the colonies, or States, were enrolled, organized, and subjected to a certain degree of discipline. From this body, in the event of a sudden emergency, a requisite force was obtained by allotment or draft. The people were deeply impressed with the severity of the burdens, and the danger to the liberties of the people incident to the maintenance of a large standing army, and adopted this system as a substitute. They preferred to give service, in the event of an emergency, through this mode, rather than to maintain at all times a large army; and as the exigencies for which this force was established would be ordinarily of short duration, the people could comply with its re-

quisitions, without materially affecting their business
or other private interests.   And when the exigency
was such as to require the service of this force for a
long period of time, it was met by a draft of a portion for a brief period, ordinarily for not more than
three months, and never exceeding nine months,
whose places were supplied at the expiration of
their period of service, by an additional draft.

At the time of the commencement of the Revolutionary War, this system was fully established and
thoroughly understood by the people; and in the
articles of Confederation of the several States, adopted in 1777, after limiting the authority of the
States to maintain regular forces in time of peace, it
is provided:

"But every State shall always keep up a well-reg-
ulated and disciplined militia, sufficiently armed and
accoutred," &c.

During the Revolutionary War, upon requisitions
from Congress, quotas of militia were from time to
time raised by draft, and furnished by the several
States, for the common cause.

At the time of the adoption of the Constitution,
therefore, there were two distinct and independent
military forces known to and understood by, the
people.

The army, or regulars, composed of men obtained
by contract, through voluntary enlistment, for long
periods of service. and the militia composed of the

body of the people capable of bearing arms, at all times enrolled, organized and disciplined, to be called out in emergencies, and for brief periods, by draft. From the time of the adoption of the Constitution to the present year, the army and the militia have been invariably raised and furnished in accordance with these established usages.

Upon the happening of exigencies which entitled the United States to the services of the militia, quotas have uniformly been called for by requisition of the President upon the Governors of the respective States, as Commanders-in-Chief of the force. It has never been claimed, even when, as in the war of 1812, the Governor of Massachusetts declined to respond to a requisition, that the United States could require the service of this force, except through the agency of the officers of the States.

The army has been, during this period, as invariably raised by voluntary enlistments. With one exception, no claim has ever been made that it could be raised through any other mode. In 1814 a sufficient force had not been obtained through enlistments, and a bill was proposed in Congress authorizing a draft upon certain contingencies. This proposition was met with the most uncompromising opposition. It was denounced in the strongest language by Daniel Webster, Jeremiah Mason, Judge Dagget, Gov. Gore, and others, as unconstitutional, and destructive of the liberties of the people.

It was defeated, and the authors of it were saved from the effects of its universal condemnation by the people, only through the cessation of excitement on the subject, which followed the immediate settlement of the war.

The reason for this distinction in the mode of raising the respective forces is obvious. It would be wholly inconsistent with the spirit of the free institutions of this country, or of England, to require the citizens to make a profession of arms, and to abandon for a term of years, their business and other important interests. It is a power which only the most absolute governments have dared to exercise.

What disposition of these two military forces did the people intend to make, in adopting the Constitution ?

They clearly intended to give the United States exclusive authority to raise and maintain the army, intending to limit its numbers in time of peace, by the provision in regard to appropriations of money to its use ; and to the respective States exclusive authority over the militia, excepting that it was to be disciplined in conformity with directions of Congress, and portions of it furnished to the United States in the event of either of the three exigencies enumerated in the Constitution. In every other respect, and for every other legitimate purpose, the militia, as a military force, was reserved to the several States,

as the guardians of their respective powers and sov
ereignties. The people were extremely jealous of
the powers given to the General Government by the
Constitution, and desired to adopt every precaution
to prevent the General Government from overriding
or absorbing the powers reserved to the States.
This is apparent, not only from the debates in the
Convention which framed it, but from the debates
in the Conventions of the people in the several
States, assembled for its ratification.

So profoundly were the people impressed with the
importance of this subject, that, although the original Constitution was sufficiently explicit, under any
proper rules of construction, upon the question of
the reserved powers of the States and their right
to maintain the militia, Congress at its first session,
upon the recommendation of different States, through
resolutions passed when they ratified the Constitution, initiated the amendments, which were subsequently adopted, asserting that "the powers not delegated to the United States by the Constitution, nor
prohibited by it to the States, are reserved to the
States respectively, or to the people," and that:

"A well regulated militia being necessary to the
security of a free State, the right of the people to
keep and bear arms shall not be infringed."

It is very clear that the people not only intended to
reserve important authority in the States, but also
the power to vindicate and protect such authority.

In the Convention of the people of Massachusetts which ratified the Constitution, the importance of these reserved rights in the States was fully discussed, and the dangers to be apprehended from the power of the United States, under the proposed Constitution amply considered.

Chief Justice Parsons was a member of the Convention, from Newburyport, and in favor of the adoption of the Constitution. In an able argument he vindicated the powers of the States under the proposed instrument. He said:

"The oath the several legislative, executive and judicial officers of the several States take to support the Federal Constitution, is as effectual a security against the usurpation of the General Government as it is against the encroachment of the State governments. For an increase of the powers by usurpation, is as clearly a violation of the Federal Constitution, as a diminution of these powers by private encroachment—and that the oath obliges the officers of the several States as vigorously to oppose the one as the other. But there is another check founded in the nature of the Union, superior to all the parchment checks that can be invented. If there should be an usurpation it will not be upon the farmer and merchant, employed and attentive only to their several occupations, it will be upon thirteen legislatures, completely organized, possessed of the confidence of the people, and having the *means* as

well as inclination, successfully to oppose it. Under
these circumstances, none but madmen would attempt
an usurpation. But, sir, the people themselves have
it in their power effectually to resist usurpation,
without being driven to an appeal to arms. An act
of usurpation is not obligatory, it is not law, and
any man may be justified in his resistance. But let
him be considered as a criminal by the General
Government, yet only his own fellow citizens can
convict him—they are his jury, and if they pronounce him innocent, not all the powers of Congress
can hurt him; and innocent they certainly will pronounce him, if the supposed law he resisted was an
act of usurpation." It may appear strange to some
that it did not occur to this eminent jurist that the
citizen in such a crisis might be deprived of the
benefits of a trial, under the plea of military necessity.

Under the Constitution, the several States have
various and important powers, entirely independent
of the control of the General Government, and
within the sphere of their exclusive jurisdictions
they are supreme to the same extent that the United
States is, in the exercise of the exclusive powers
with which it is clothed.

If States or the people undertake to obstruct the
lawful authority of the United States Government,
that Government is invested with a power, and it
becomes its duty, to forcibly protect its authority,

and if the United States Government attempts to usurp any of the powers of the States, or to illegally interfere with the rights of their citizens, they have a force under their command, and it becomes their duty, to defend their threatened rights and authority.

The success of our system of Government has always depended, and must always depend, upon the strict maintenance of the equilibrium of authorities created and recognized by the Constitution. If the authority of the United States shall be overthrown, then the whole system falls to the ground; and if the powers of the States shall be wrested from them, the same catastrophe must follow. It is indispensable for the safety of our institutions, that those representing the respective powers established by the Constitution jealously guard those powers against all encroachments. Our institutions and our liberties are to be preserved by performing, and requiring performance of, all the obligations imposed by the Constitution, and not by any reliance upon the infallibility of men.

Men, however honest we may believe them to be, may change or be changed. The tendency of power is never to curtail, but invariably to extend its prerogatives. This is a necessary result of the principles of man's nature. and the best men are not proof against this influence. Therefore, those in power are never impartial judges upon the question of the just limits of their authority. It is only through independent tribunals that its limits can be properly defined, and through the remonstrance of those who must suffer from its encroachments, and have the power to resist, that it is to be restrained within its legitimate boundaries.

Such is a brief sketch of the history of the army and the militia—of the established usages in the employment of each—of the distribution of these forces under the Constitution, and the importance of these distributions to the preservation of our political system.

It is now important to enquire, whether, independent of questions of expediency, Congress has authority under the Constitution, to require, by compulsion, the service of the body of the people in the army, or national forces of the United States.

No rules of construction, applicable to the limited powers of the General Government, in the absence of express provisions prescribing the mode of raising armies, will authorize a departure from existing modes, established by long and invariable usage, especially when such an innovation cannot be executed without seriously affecting the dearest and most important personal rights of the people.

The usages in regard to the raising of armies, as has been shown, had been uniform, for centuries before the adoption of the Constitution, and the construction of the sections of the Constitution authorizing this force, has been for nearly eighty years under that instrument, strictly in accordance with these usages.

But, further, the Constitution practically takes from the United States the power to require the military service of the body of the people in the army, through compulsion, in its clear and uncontroverted provisions regarding the militia. It specially recognizes the existence of this force, and provides for its maintenance. This force could never be materially affected by voluntary enlistments in the army; but if the United States has authority to compel the body of the people, who compose the militia, into the army; is it not clearly a power which may be entirely destructive of the militia, and consequently of the power of the States?

Therefore, the claim on the part of Congress of an authority to draft the body of the people into the Federal Army, is not only without any express authority in the Constitution, and opposed to established usages, but can only be carried into practical effect through such encroachments upon the established usages upon which another and important force is established by the Constitution, in which the several States have an independent and vital interest, as to practically destroy that force.

But it is asserted by some, that the Constitution may be construed to admit of a concurrent power in the United States and the several States, over the body of the people for their respective forces. ˥ This claim is equally unsupported by express grant, usage, or our practice under the Constitution. It is also clearly impossible, from the nature of things, that any such authority could have been intended. It is an assertion that the people intended to give concurrent power to two governments, over the same persons, which would inevitably result in direct conflict. If the United States has concurrent power with the respective States to enroll and draft the body of the people, the one into the army and the other into the militia, and in the exercise of it both make a draft, and the same person or persons are drawn by both authorities, which will have the paramount right? Or will it be claimed that the authority which first drafts the individual will be entitled to his service? If this is so, and a conflict between the two authorities should spring up, a simultaneous attempt would be made to secure the force. If the United States should order a draft of the entire body, and perfect it in advance of the State, where, then, is the power of the State, and its militia? and if the State should be in advance of the General Government in the draft, what has become of the power of the General Government over the men it has enrolled? It is absurd to suppose that any such dangerous concurrent power could have been intended.

It is further asserted, under the fashionable doctrines that have of late been prevalent, that the necessities of the present exigency authorize the exercise of such extraordinary power. No more pernicious or dangerous doctrine was ever entertained by a free people. But if this doctrine were admissible, is it supported by the facts? The power to enlarge the army by increased pay or bounties, is not exhausted. The United States Government has a right to require the aid of the militia to an indefinite extent, which, reasoning from past experience in this war, and upon the presumptions arising from legal obligation, will be promptly furnished upon requisition. The people will readily respond to a call to this s ervice, as they will feel it is a duty they clearly owe to the Government. They will not feel oppressed by the demand. as they know the limits of that service, and that they can perform their obligations in the company of their neighbors and friends, and under officers from their vicinage, who will feel a personal interest and ambition in their comfort and welfare. They will also feel, that in the event of an illegal demand by the United States, or an attempt to exercise an unauthorized power over them, they can rely upon the authorities of their State for protection. Besides, the militia is the very force especially provided by the Constitution for such an exigency as the present. Blackstone, in the extract above quoted, says of the militia, in England:

"This is the constitutional security which our laws have provided for the public peace, and for protecting the realm against foreign or domestic violence."

The militia in this country is the constitutional security which our Constitution has provided for the public peace, and for protecting the Government against foreign and domestic violence. So long as it exists can it be said that there is an exigency for a military force which the Constitution has not provided for?

Independent of the service of the militia, under the extraordinary calls that have been made on the people for voluntary enlistments during the past two years, there has been such a ready and willing response as was never before made in this, or in any other country. Why, then, is it to be assumed that the same spirit will not continue? Is it because a majority of the people believe that the principles upon which the war is being waged by the administration, will prove destructive of our institutions? If so, then the administration should defer to the will of the people. No war should be waged by an administration, in a republic, against the opinions of a majority of the people. Is it upon the ground that the administration intends, upon the principles it has asserted, to prosecute the war on such an unprecedented and gigantic scale, that the modes established by the wisdom of the past fail of meeting its requirements? Then is it not its duty to consult, instead of compelling, the people? Is it for the purpose of consolidating all power, civil and military, in the United States, regardless of the constitutional rights of the States? If so the people will never permit it.

The modes of raising military forces provided by the Constitution are sufficient for the prosecution of any war that ought to be prosecuted, and an Administration takes upon itself a fearful responsibility, and one for which in the end it must answer to the people, when, in its own discretion, it oversteps the bounds prescribed by the fathers for the protection of the liberties of the people, and compels by its power, the citizen to perform a military service, which the Constitution and laws do not require.

The powers asserted in the Conscription Act are clear and intelligible. In the first section it is provided,

"That all able-bodied male citizens of the United States, and persons of foreign birth who shall have declared on oath their intention to become citizens under and in pursuance of the laws thereof, between the ages of twenty and forty-five years, except as hereinafter excepted, are hereby declared to constitute the national forces, and shall be liable to perform military duty in the service of the United States when called out by the President for that purpose."

In section eleven it is provided,

"That all persons thus enrolled shall be subject for two years after the first day of July succeeding the enrollment, to be called into the military service of the United States, and to continue in service during the present rebellion, not however exceeding the term of three years."

In section thirty-four it is provided,

"That all persons drafted under the provisions of this Act shall be assigned by the President to military duty in such corps, regiments, or other branches of the service, as the exigencies of the service may require."

Now, what is the authority asserted in this act? Under it Congress has not claimed, in terms, the right to compel the service of the militia as such, independent of State agencies; nor has it claimed the right, in terms, to compel militia men, as such, into the army of the United States. These would have been too plainly expressed usurpations of power. But the act does assert the right in Congress to enrol every man of the militia, in every State of the Union, in the National force, and to compel his service in the army of the United States.

The militia is repeatedly recognized in the act itself, and reference is made to the services of this force in the present war; yet the act asserts authority in the United States to take, by force, every enrolled militia man in the country, and compel him into the exclusive service of the United States, as a member of the national force or army.

This act is an assertion of a right in the United States to completely annihilate the militia of the

States—to leave the States as such entirely power-less and defenceless. If authoritative, it is a virtual and complete destruction of all State authority and power. It leaves to the several States the empty form of a government, shorn of all power in itself of enforcing its laws, protecting its citizens, or resist-ing unlawful demands from abroad. The assertion does not even admit a concurrent power in the States. No reservation whatever is made of the militia or any portion of them. With one fell swoop they are all gathered up in the several States, and forcibly transferred to the exclusive authority of the United States.

# DOES THE BIBLE SANCTION AMERICAN SLAVERY?*

WE have read, with much interest, a book written by Goldwin Smith, more than a year since, upon the question, Does the Bible sanction American Slavery? also an able article sustaining the views of the author, published in the last January number of the *North American Review.*

Goldwin Smith is a professor in Oxford University, England, and a member of the most intellectual class of the school of philanthropists. The *North American Review* is an able exponent of the anti-slavery sentiment of this country.

The theories laid down in the book are in the main sound, the admissions of principles clear and distinct, and but few of the deductions of the author are open to criticism, except from the poverty or unsoundness of the statements of facts on which they are based.

* Does the Bible sanction American Slavery? By Goldwin Smith. Cambridge : Sever & Francis. 1863.

Review of the above-entitled book of Goldwin Smith, in the *North American Review,* January, 1864.

Published in the *American Monthly Magazine,* January, 1865

The admissions of both these writers are entitled
to great consideration, for. if true, they determine
grave questions, upon which the minds of large numbers of our people have been perplexed in the attention they have given to the subject.

There are many persons at the North who con-
scientiously believe that slavery, or the involuntary
personal subordination of one man to another, or of
one class of men to another, is prohibited by the
Bible; and that, consequently, it is necessarily sinful
for one man, under any circumstances, to hold
another in slavery.   There are others at the North
who, admitting that slavery is not, under all circumstances, forbidden by the Bible as sinful, yet consci-
entiously believe that the system of servitude. as it
exists in the Southern States, is based upon a gross
violation of divine laws.   Under these convictions,
with erroneous views of their relations to, and responsibility for, the supposed wrong under our system of government, both classes attempt to justify
themselves in subordinating every other considera.
tion and interest to that of eradicating from the
country this sinful system.

We believe that no accurate student of the Bible
will contend that slavery is therein forbidden, and
no one with a knowledge of mankind, and of God's
providences and His dealings with humanity, will
come rationally to the conclusion that the holding
of human beings in involuntary servitude is, neces-

sarily, and under all circumstances, a transgression of any of God's general laws.

It is of primary importance to determine upon the correctness or falsity of these propositions, before we proceed to a consideration of the rightfulness or wrongfulness of any particular system of slavery. Because, if slavery is necessarily and under all circumstances sinful, then no system founded on it can, under any circumstances, be justified. But if slavery, under some circumstances, and with certain limitations, is not sinful, then it becomes important, in the consideration of any particular system, to first examine and ascertain in what respects, if any, it transcends the boundaries of human expediency. and trenches upon the immutable principles of the divine laws.

Does, then, the Bible forbid slavery, or is the involuntary personal subordination of one man to another sinful, under all circumstances?

Under the Levitical law, the Hebrews were expressly authorized to hold slaves. They were restricted by that law in the enslavement of their own people, the children of Israel, who were the chosen people of God. The command was: "Both thy bondmen and thy bondmaids, which thou shalt have, shall be of the heathen that are round about you: of them shall ye buy bondmen and bondmaids. Moreover, of the children of the strangers that do sojourn among you, of them shall ye buy, and of their families that are with you, which they begat in your land; and they shall be your possession. And ye shall take them as an inheritance for your children after you, to inherit them for a possession; they shall be your bondmen forever: but over your brethren, the children of Israel, ye shall not rule over one another with rigor." Under this law the Hebrews held slaves, and Abraham himself had servants not only "born in his house," but "bought with his money." This system was continued through all the nations of antiquity, and existed in Greece and Rome in the time of Christ and His apostles. Christ did not at any time attempt to interfere with the system, and nowhere forbade it. He recognized the political and social institutions which existed in the world based upon the fact of the inequalities of the human race. He interfered with none of them. He proposed no system to regulate the affairs of society, or the relations between men. His mission was to the individual, to improve and elevate him, through the silent and beneficent influences of the religion He taught. His object was the gradual advancement of mankind, and a consequent modification of systems and correction of abuses.

The teachings of the Bible upon the subject of slavery are plainly admitted by Professor Smith. He says:

"It is true that the Old Testament distinctly recognizes slavery as a Hebrew institution. It is also true that the New Testament speaks of slavery in several passages, and does not condemn it."

Upon the question whether all men are entitled to political and personal liberty, Professor Smith says:

" The authors of the Declaration of Independence, on which the American Constitution for the Slave as well the Free States is founded, say : ' We hold these truths to be self-evident : that all men are created equal ; that they are endowed by their Creator with certain unalienable rights ; that among these are life, liberty, and the pursuit of happiness ; and that to secure these rights, governments are instituted among men, deriving their just powers from the consent of the governed.' Supposing the negro to be a man, the slave-owners who have set their hands to these sentiments have pronounced the doom of their own institution, and saved its adversaries further trouble. But it must, in fairness to them, be owned that they have set their hands to too much. It can scarcely be held that liberty, political or personal, is the inalienable right of every human being. Children possess neither political nor personal liberty till they arrive at what the law, a law which they had no share in making, pronounces to be years of discretion. Women have no political liberties, and married women have personal liberties only of a very qualified kind. Under despotic governments, the immorality of which can scarcely be held in all cases self-evident, no one has political liberty. Even under constitutional governments, where the suffrage is limited, as it is to some extent in most of those which are commonly called free countries, the unenfranchised classes are as destitute of political liberty as the subjects of a despotism. The political power which commands their obedience is vested, it is true, in a great number of hands, and is on that account more controlled by the influence of opinions, and less liable to gross abuse ; but it commands their obedience as absolutely and as irrespectively of their own consent, as though it were that of a despotic prince. The equality between man and man on which this indefeasible claim to political and personal liberty is founded, is in truth rather a metaphysical notion than a fact.'"

Upon the same subject, the writer in the *North American Review* says:

" Servitude, therefore, or the subjection of man to man, does not contradict the laws of nature. It represents the relation of weakness to strength. It has existed in all nations at some period of their growth. The condition of its presence is the existence of a class unfit to enjoy personal liberty, or the want of power in government to protect the rights of individuals ; for personal liberty is a right for those who can use it without injury to themselves or others. In the former case, personal liberty may be denied or restricted by law, and according to the necessity for that law, its humanity and justice, will the government that makes it be judged."

And further :

" There are two kinds of liberty—political and personal. The former consists in a share of political power. To gain it, to keep it, and to exercise it for the the good of society, implies a degree of intelligence never possessed by a barbarous people, and by certain classes only of the more civilized. As nations advance in wealth and knowledge, this intelligence is more largely diffused. Intelligence means the power to think, and thinking produces the desire for action. . . Political liberty, therefore, a power over the conduct of government, is enjoyed now, as always, by a very small proportion of mankind. . . To be governed by the few, in all public affairs, is and always has been the lot of a vast majority of men. . . . Personal liberty is the power which a man has over himself, over his own actions and destiny, so far as these are not controlled by general laws affecting the whole community. Intelligence, combined with moral force—what is called ability—is the condition on which this sort of liberty can be enjoyed ; for power is the inseparable attribute of ability, and loss of power of the want of it. Personal liberty is thus, like political liberty, the boon of advancing civilization, because civilization, by increasing the objects of desire and effort, stimulates and exercises varied talent."

If we assume, then, that involuntary personal subordination is not necessarily sinful, but that, under certain conditions and restrictions, it may be justifiable, the questions which arise in relation to slavery in the Southern States are:

*First.*—Do the circumstances and position of the two races, the Caucasian and the African, at the South, render the personal subordination of the latter to the former justifiable?

*Second.*—If such subordination is justifiable, then, is the system of servitude that exists at the South justifiable, and such as the Bible will sanction?

*Third.*—Are there any abuses connected with the system and not necessary to its existence, that can be prevented by law, that are wrongful?

Upon the first question, the facts are, that, in the words of the writer in the *North American Review*, "we have in this country four millions of negroes. They are of a race inferior to ours;" they are distributed through the States of the South, comprising, in some States, more than one half, and in all a considerable portion, of their populations; they are not only of an inferior race, but devoid of civilization, except what they have attained to since their transportation to this country. Under these circumstances, what policy, consistent with right, will promote the highest interests and happiness of both races, and best advance the welfare of the society which they constitute? Will a policy which imposes upon the inferior race no other political or personal restraints than are imposed upon the white population, compass these ends? Experience and reason

teach us they will not. The negroes have not arrived at that stage of progress from which they can
be expected to advance with a self-evolving civilization; and if left to themselves and the laws enacted
for the whites alone, they will inevitably relapse into
the state of barbarism from which they have just
commenced to emerge; they will be governed by the
lower passions of uncivilized races, will not respect
or be governed by the laws of civilized society, will
commit depredations, and become addicted to habits
of indolence and vagrancy. If the assertions of the
writer in the *North American Review* are correct,
that " personal liberty is the boon of advancing civilization," and is only a right " for those who can
use it without injury to themselves or others," does
our knowledge of the negroes of the South justify
the belief that, if left to themselves, they will use
their acquired liberty without injury to themselves
or others? We believe it does not. Our experience
with the freedmen, as the enfranchised negroes at
the South are styled, since the commencement of the
present war, has furnished most important corrobo-
ration of this belief. The testimony of the officers
who have had command in the several departments
in which slaves in large numbers have been freed,
has been uniform upon the subject.

General Hunter, whilst in command in South Carolina, in an order for a draft of all the able-bodied
negroes in his department, said:

" No more efficient means of elevating the former bondmen from their degraded condition to the civilized status of the white race can be devised than the schooling they will receive in the army."

He also referred to military discipline as "the best prevention of any abuse of their just attained freedom."

General Banks early saw the necessity of the personal subordination of the freedmen, and in a general order, dated January 29th, 1863, he provided that—

" Those who leave their employers will be compelled to support themselves and families by labor upon the public works. Under no circumstances whatever can they be maintained in idleness, or allowed to wander through the parishes and cities without employment. Vagrancy and crime will be suppressed by an enforced and constant occupation and employment."

The above are extracts from some of the many orders that have been issued in the different departments, showing the convictions of those in command of the necessity of the personal subordination of the freedmen, for the protection of society and the public interest, even in districts occupied by our armies. But these acts and expressions have not been confined to the generals in the field. The Federal Administration has been governed in its policy toward the negroes by the inexorable logic of the truths which its experience with the race has taught, and in all its dealings with them has acknowledged the necessity for their personal subordination.

If, then, the condition of the negroes and their relations to society, at the South, are such as to render the personal subordination of the race necessary and proper, is the system of servitude which exists in that section justifiable, and such as the Bible can sanction ?

In the consideration of this question we shall refer only to the fundamental principles of the system, essential to its existence, which are involved in the ownership by the master of the personal services of the slave, and the reciprocal obligations and duties which the system has imposed upon the master, leaving the consideration of incidental provisions connected with. but not necessary to the continuance of the system, to be discussed in another connection.

Is, then, this system, upon the facts that have been stated. wrongful ? not, are there abuses connected with it which should be relieved ? but is the system, the mode of subordination itself, a wrongful one ?   Not to go back of our own experience, the system which exists at the South is the same which has prevailed in this country from the time of its first settlement.   It is the only system that has ever existed at the South, and the precise system under which slaves were held at the North for more than a century.   Less than a century ago it was discontinued at the North, but plainly upon the ground that its continuance would not promote the material interests of the section. The laws for its prohibition at the North were in each instance prospective, thereby affording an.opportunity to owners of slaves to dispose of them in States where the system was to be continued; which could not have been done if the reason of the discontinuance was the moral wrong of the system. Whilst the system was permitted at the North, it was approved of not only by the more mercenary and irreligious classes, but by the best men in the communities where it was maintained. One hundred years ago there were few clergymen at the North, of sufficient means, who did not own one or more slaves; and is it a violent presumption that the same class to-day would own servants, " bought with their money," if the system had continued to be beneficial to the material interests of the North? Few men will contend that the clergymen of the different religious denominations at the South to-day are not true and sincere Christians. Yet we find them all strongly approving of the system as it exists in their section. From " An Address to Christians throughout the world, by a Convention of Ministers assembled at Richmond, Virginia, April, 1863," signed by ninety-six clergymen of the different denominations, many of them heretofore known as among the most eminent divines of the country, we give the following extract:

" We are aware that in respect to the moral aspects of slavery, we differ from those who conceive of emancipation as a measure of benevolence, and on that account we suffer much reproach which we are conscious of not deserving. With all the facts of the system of slavery, in its practical operations, before us, 'as eye-witnesses and ministers of the Word, having had perfect understanding of all things' on this subject of which we speak, we may surely claim respect for our opinions and statements. Most of us have grown up from childhood among the slaves; all of us have preached to and taught them the Word of Life; have administered to them the ordinances of the Christian Church; sincerely love them as souls for whom Christ died; we go among them freely, and know them in health and sickness, in labor and rest, from infancy to old age. We are familiar with their physical and moral condition, and alive to all their interests; and we testify, in the sight of God, that the relation of master and slave among us, however we may deplore abuses in this, as in other relations of mankind, is not incompatible with our holy Christianity, and that the presence of the African in our land is an occasion of gratitude on their behalf before God; seeing that thereby Divine Providence has brought them where missionaries of the Cross may freely proclaim to them the word of salvation, and the work is not interrupted by agitating fanaticism. The South has done more than any people on earth for the Christianization of the African race The condition of the slave here is not wretched, as Northern fictions would have men believe, but prosperous and happy, and would have been yet more so but for the mistaken zeal of the abolitionists. Can emancipation obtain for them a better portion? The practicable plan for benefiting the African race must be the providential plan—the Scriptural plan. We adopt that plan in the South, and while the States would seek by wholesome legislation to regard the interest of master and slave, we, as ministers, would preach the Word to both, as we are commanded of God. This war has not benefited the slaves. Those who have been encouraged or compelled by the enemy to leave their masters have gone, and we aver can go, to no state of society that offers them any better things than they have at home, either in respect to their temporal or eternal welfare."

We do not claim that the fact that the system of slavery which exists in this country has been uniformly approved of by the best men in the communities where it has existed, necessarily proves that the system is a rightful one. But when, upon a thorough knowledge of the practical operations of a system, the best men in the community where it exists can see nothing in it to condemn, that fact is an important one to be taken into consideration in determining upon the question of its sinfulness. It will hardly be contended that the prevailing sentiment of a community, or mere private interest, can so far control the judgment and blind the eyes of the spiritual guides of the world, that, through successive generations, they can be induced to approve of palpably sinful practices.

But, if the personal subordination of the negroes at the South is necessary, can any better system be devised for the purpose than the one which exists at the South? The Federal Administration has passed a sentence of condemnation against the system, and the war has been directed, the last two years, for its overthrow. It has proposed a new system as a sub. stitute for it. Is this system more beneficial to society, or to either race, than the one it would supplant? This system is based upon the letting out of negroes to white masters for limited periods of service, giving to the master personal control over the negro. We cannot conceive of any advantages to society, or the white race, from the new system over the old. The personal subordination

is as effective under the one as the other. But the
operations of the old system, shorn of its abuses, we
believe to be far more beneficial to the negro than
the new. In the permanent relations which are
maintained under the old system, strong and mutual
attachments and sympathies are necessarily created
between the master and the slave, greatly to the
advantage of the latter. Prof. Smith says that:
"To the Hebrew slave, the fact that he was his
master's money, would always be a real though not
always a sufficient protection." So to the Southern
slave, the fact that he is his master's money affords
to him the strongest guaranty against injury from
his master. The value of the slave to his master
depends upon the amount of labor he performs, and
the cheerfulness with which he performs it. It is
evident that kindness and generous treatment on
the part of the master will best promote these ends.
If the slave is sick or disabled, his master not only
loses the benefit of his labor, but is obliged by law
to support him. The legal obligations of the master
are to care for and support the slave in health, in
sickness, and in old age. These mutual obligations
tend to mutual regard and kindness. In judging of
the probable operations of such a system, we should
keep in mind known principles of man's nature.
Services faithfully performed by the slave naturally
induce sentiments of generosity and forbearance on
the part of the master. The precise results of any

theoretical system cannot be understood without an opportunity for accurate observations upon its practical workings. We know that, as a class, the negroes of the South have been happy and contented in their condition under the system that exists. The anticipations of those at the North, that the slaves were panting for enfranchisement from the system, have not been realized. We have found in our experience in the war, that, notwithstanding the inducements offered and assistance tendered to the slaves to achieve their liberties, but comparatively few have made the attempt, and there has been, in no instance, a servile insurrection.

It cannot be expected that such mutual attachments and sympathies will spring up between the freedmen and their masters, under the system of subordination adopted by the Administration. Under this system the negroes are let for limited periods of service. The system appeals only to the selfish nature of the master. With him it is solely a matter of contract, from which he is looking only for immediate pecuniary gain. The master has no responsibility for the condition of the slave beyond his term of service, and his object is to secure the largest amount of labor from him within the prescribed time. Not only theoretically but practically, we believe the new system to be antagonistic to the interests and happiness of the negro. One of the most radical of the anti-slavery papers of the country,\* at the close of an able article upon the practical workings of the new system, says: "It is serfdom more galling than any that ever existed under the old system, and to call it anything else is hypocrisy."

In the July number of the *North American Review*, the great disappointment of those who, before the war, believed the negro at the South was anxious of relieving himself of the system, is plainly manifested. The *Review* speaks of movements " in defence of liberties of blacks who can show no better title to them than the at least doubtful one of a measure of " military necessity ; " and further :

"It might be different if the negroes were men of a sterner mould and a more indomitable spirit, men who not simply desired freedom, but hated oppressors. But it must be confessed that their apathy during the present struggle has disappointed both their friends and enemies. The tameness with which they suffer themselves to be assassinated, to be carried back into bondage and held in it, and with which they have submitted to every other outrage which either party chooses to inflict upon them, may be proof either of sublime patience or of extreme degradation; but in either case it indicates a state of mind which, though it may have spared us some embarrassment during the war, promises to throw serious obstacles in the way of their redemption after the restoration of peace. Some trace of self-respect, even if it take the low form of savage vindictiveness, is the first condition of moral and social elevation. When it fails to reveal itself in a whole race, and when this race has to assert its claims to mere manhood against oppressors of such a fierce and vigorous type as the Southern slaveholder, it is hard to say how much third parties can do to help it."

\* The *Boston Commonwealth.*

We do not understand that Professor Smith claims that the system of personal subordination at the South, with the qualifications we have stated, is wrongful. He arrives at certain conclusions, based upon abuses of the system, which we shall consider in their proper connections. He states that "slavery in Greece and Rome may in the earliest times have been a social necessity and a sound relation, as it was in the patriarchal East." The systems of Greece and Rome permitted the enslavement not only of the inhabitants of surrounding nations, but of the weaker and more unfortunate classes of their own people. Their slaves consisted of captives taken in war or obtained by piracy and kidnapping, and of citizens sentenced to servitude for crime or debt, and the master had absolute power of life and death over the slave.

If Professor Smith can justify such a system of slavery in the earlier times of Greece and Rome, he could hardly denounce as sinful the system for the subordination of a confessedly inferior race, which exists at the South, or claim that " social necessity " may not render the relation it creates "a sound relation."

If the system of personal subordination at the South, with the qualifications we have stated, may be morally justifiable, are there any abuses connected with it, and not necessary to its existence, which can be prevented by law, which are wrongful?

We believe there are. A considerable portion of
the book of Professor Smith is filled with statements
of abuses to which, under the laws of the slave
States, the system is liable, and with repetitions of
the stories of instances of cruelty of slaveholders,
which have been from time to time reported. Upon
the strength of these, elaborately set forth, Professor
Smith comes to the conclusion, in which the writer
in the *North American Review* concurs, that we can
find no sanction for *American* slavery in the record
of Christianity in the Bible; but, instead of advo-
cating a reform of these abuses and wrongs, upon
which their conclusion is based, both writers fall into
the current of the radical anti-slavery sentiment of
this country, in favor of a revolutionary policy.
Such a policy is entirely inconsistent with the admissions they both make, of the social necessity of
the personal subordination of people unfit to enjoy
personal liberty, when introduced in considerable
numbers, to remain, in the society of others fitted to
enjoy this privilege.

The writer in the *North American Review* says, in
regard to the negroes at the South:

"We are told, also, that they are unfit to enjoy personal liberty,
to exercise power individually over themselves, to be governed each
by his own will under the law. Is this true? Let us grant it.
What, then, is the duty of the superior race which has power over
the negro? Does not the possession of this power, by every principle of justice and humanity, make it a trustee for the negro?
What is meant when it is said the negro is unfit for personal liber-

ty ? Is it not that he is unable to take care of himself, that he ret
quires a care-taker, a guide, a support, as a child does? Are no-
those, therefore, who have power over him, who claim and take
that power, bound to furnish the guardianship he needs for *his*
benefit, and, since his conduct and condition affect their interests,
for their own also ! "

He grants, what he nowhere else disputes, that
the negroes of the South are now unfit to enjoy personal liberty, and yet, inferentially at least, approves
of the abolition of the system in existence at the
South, without proposing any other system as a substitute for it, or even a scheme for the government
of the negroes, when freed.

The prominent opportunities of abuse by the master under the system, from which it is claimed that
the negro may be deprived of rights and benefits
which he is entitled to under the relation, arise from
want of adequate legal provisions for the education
of the slaves, and for the prevention of violations of
the marriage relations, and of the separation of families. Although it is not to be inferred that, because
there is a power of abuse, the power is necessarily
exercised, yet, in a system affecting the highest interests of so large a class of human beings, it is the
duty of the Government to prevent possibilities of
abuse, to the extent of its legitimate power. The
liability to abuse in the particulars above-named can
be prevented by legislation, and it is the duty of the
legislatures in the States where the system is permitted, to make sufficient provisions for the purpose.

This subject, we have reason to believe, has engaged the serious attention of the best men at the South. The Pastoral Address of the Bishops of the Episcopal Church in the South, issued at Augusta, Georgia, in November, 1862, urges upon the people of that section the duty of giving to the slaves that moral and religious instruction which is to elevate them in the scale of being, and says:

"It is likewise the duty of the Church to press upon the masters of the country their obligations, as Christian men, so to arrange this institution as not to necessitate the violation of those sacred relations which God has created, and which men cannot, consistently with Christian duty, annul. The systems of labor which prevail in Europe, and which are, in many respects, more severe than ours, are so arranged as to prevent all necessity for the separation of parents and children, and of husbands and wives; and a very little care on our part would rid the system upon which we are about to plant our national life, of these unchristian features. It belongs, especially, to the Episcopal Church to urge a proper teaching upon this subject, for in her fold and congregations are found a very large proportion of the great slaveholders of the country. We rejoice to be able to say that the public sentiment is rapidly becoming sound upon this subject, and that the legislatures of several of the Confederate States have already taken steps toward this great consummation."

That there will be opportunities for abuse under the system, with all the protection which human laws can afford, there can be no doubt; and this can be said, to a greater or lesser extent, of every system adopted to control the relations of men with each other. Under the system for the personal subordination of children to parents, and wives to husbands, there have been not unfrequent instances of fiendish cruelty and crime. Yet these instances have been exceptional, and because they have occurred, no one advocates the abolition of the systems, or believes them to be sinful.

We must deal with mankind as we find it. We cannot expect perfection in this world, nor should we attempt to revolutionize systems founded on the necessities of our natures or relations, solely because, under them, there are possibilities, or even instances, of abuse. If we should, but few systems could survive the test. Our duties, under the beneficent principles of our Christian religion, are to reform, and not to revolutionize—to improve and perfect systems and institutions, by protecting them, so far as possible, from opportunity of abuse, by the laws of the State; and from abuses which the law cannot reach, by educating the minds of the people, and inculcating in their hearts the ennobling sentiments of justice and humanity. The brotherhood of man is an idea which has been long striven after, but never realized. It is toward this that the principles of Christianity tend. In a struggle of eighteen hundred years, we can note progress; yet, when we look forward to the great consummation,

> "The wide, the unbounded prospect lies before us,
> But shadows, clouds, and darkness rest upon it."

It may not appear plain to us why a good God,

in His infinite wisdom, has created men and races differing in capacities and condition, and has not given to all the same opportunities for worldly happiness and prosperity. But these distinctions and varieties exist, and must be necessarily recognized in the social systems which are organized for the protection and advancement of society.

It is with the moral questions of a system based upon such distinctions, we have attempted to deal. We have not considered the question of the moral responsibility of those who brought the negro to this country. Prof. Smith says: "The position into which the piratical cupidity of the whites has brought the two races at the South is an awkward one." We grant it. But who were guilty of this piratical cupidity? It was the policy of England that forced the negro to our shores, and her power that maintained the slave trade between the colonies and Africa, even against the remonstrances of the colonists. In 1760, South Carolina passed an act prohibiting the further importation of African slaves. The act was not only rejected by the Crown, but the Governor was reprimanded, and the Governors of all the colonies warned, by royal edict, against countenancing similar legislation; and even as late as in 1775, in answer to a remonstrance from the colonies, upon the subject, the Premier of England replied: "We cannot allow the colonies to check or discourage in any degree a traffic so beneficial to

the nation." But whatever the share our fathers
may have had in the responsibility of transporting
the negroes here, certainly the white population of
the South, of this generation, has not contributed to
the wrong. It found in its midst a numerous people of an inferior race, unfitted for personal liberty,
and for whose expatriation no adequate, practicable
plan had ever been proposed, and it continued the
system of subordination which it found in operation,
which had been sanctioned by the fathers of both
sections. "The position" into which "the piratical
cupidity of the whites" has brought the two races
at the South may be not only "an awkward one,"
but an unfortunate one, for the highest interests of
the white population and the progress of society in
that section. But the position, however awkward,
is one that, under one system or another, must be
endured, unless the negroes are exterminated, or
some feasible mode of effectual colonization shall be
devised.

We believe that, not by revolutionary, but by re-
formatory and truly philanthropic efforts, the institution of slavery at the South will be shorn of its
worst abuses, the negro gradually improved and
lifted in the scale of being, and the condition of his
practical relations with the white race modified
until, in the fulness of time, if it shall be proved he
is capable of such advancement, he will be fitted for,
and will inevitably enjoy, the boon of personal liberty.

# THE CAUSE OF OUR STRIFE AND THE REMEDY.*

EVERY reader of American history must be impressed with the marked distinctions which have existed, from the first settlement of the country to the present time, between the people of the two great sections, the North and the South. These distinctions were plainly to be seen long before the Colonies declared their independence of Great Britain; they were marked during the war of the Revolution, and the period which immediately succeeded it; they were fully acknowledged in the Convention which framed the Constitution; and have been more signally manifested since, with the increase of the population and growth of the material interests of the respective sections.

A careful study of the history of the two people—for such they certainly have been and are in most important characteristics—will disclose the plainest evidence of such prominent and influential differences of interests and character, as would naturally and without the intervention of the American system

* Published in the *American Monthly Magazine*, April, 1865.

of government, have led to their organization into two separate and independent nationalities.

There have also been developed at the West, with the spread of population over its vast and fertile prairies, especially within the last thirty years, although not such decisive, yet prominent characteristics, distinguishing its people from those of either of the other sections; and more recently the settlement of the region west of the Rocky Mountains is disclosing yet another germ of independent interests and character.

These facts, if facts they are, should be carefully considered at all times by the statesmen of the country, and never more carefully than at a juncture like the present, when the people of one great section, through an apprehension that its great and distinguishing interests and characteristics were to be subordinated to the will of the majority of the people of other sections of the country, is engaged in a terrible struggle to assert its independence, and to establish for itself a separate nationality.

Recognizing those differences between the people of the South and the other sections, which are universally acknowledged, it is important for us to ascertain whether they have been created by circumstances which may be controlled or modified, or whether they have grown up from natural causes, which no human power is capable of restraining.

The distinctions between the people of the two

sections are manifested in the difference of their interests, occupations, sentiments, manners, customs, and institutions. What caused these differences? Judge Story, in a dissertation upon the origin of nations, in his work on International Law, says:

" Climate and geographical position, and the physical adaptations springing from them, must at all times have had a powerful influence in the organization of each society, and have given a peculiar complexion and character to many of its arrangements. The bold, intrepid, and hardy natives of the north of Europe, whether civilized or barbarous, would scarcely desire or tolerate the indolent inactivity and lascivious indulgences of the Asiatics. Nations inhiabting the borders of the ocean, and accustomed to maritime intercourse with other nations, would naturally require institutions and laws, adapted to their pursuits and enterprises, which would be wholly unfit for those who should be placed in the interior of a continent, and should maintain very different relations with their neighbors, both in peace and war."

We believe that all the essential differences between the people of the South and the other sections have arisen, principally from the first of the two causes above stated, namely, climate; and that all the essential differences between the people of the West and of the Pacific coast and the other sections, had their origin, principally, in the second cause above stated, namely, geographical position.

We propose to consider briefly, how far climate has been influential in creating the differences which exist between the people of the South and those of the other sections.

The territory of the United States, extending

through sixteen degrees of latitude, reaches at the North to a climate colder than that of the northern portion of Prussia, and at the South to a climate scarcely less tropical than that of the extreme south of Spain or Portugal. From an early day sectional divisions have been recognized, corresponding with these differences of climate: The States have been classed as Northern and Southern. In the first-named class are included all the States of the cold, and in the second, all the States of the warm climate. A still further distinction has been recognized, in the designation of the northern tier of States of the southern section, as the Border States. This distinction corresponds with the phenomena of climate, as in the gradual transition from a cold to a warm country there must necessarily be found an intermediate region, partaking somewhat of the climate of both, with none of the marked characteristics of either.

This dissimilarity in climate has been the cause of the difference in the agricultural productions of the two sections, and has exerted a powerful influence upon the character and conditions of the labor of the two people. Under a climate like that of the North, it is impossible for the laboring classes to obtain the comforts of life without constant exertion. The sterility of the soil of that section, and the length of its winters, in which the laboring classes are prevented from working in the field, naturally induce

them to seek other employments. Hence a large
portion of the population of the North, especially in
the seaboard States, have sought occupation in the
laborious employments of commerce and manufactures.

Under a climate like that of the South, with a soil
of extreme fertility, with none of the necessities
which long inclement seasons create, the laboring
classes are enabled to support themselves by agricultural pursuits, with little exertion; and thus, independent of the enervating influences of climate, but
little incentive is presented for engaging in the more
skilful and laborious employments.

At the South, commercial and manufacturing interests must always be subordinate to the agricultural, and at the North, until the further developments of the dominant interests of the Western
and Pacific States, commercial and manufacturing
interests must predominate.

But the influence of climate is shown in the difference of temperament, customs, and institutions of
the two people, scarcely less than in their labor and
productions. These differences have been plainly
observable from the time of the earliest history of
the country, and have not been materially influenced
by any differences in the characters of those who
colonized the respective sections. Both sections
were settled principally by people of the same race,
and from the same nation. There certainly was no

greater difference of characteristics in the settlers of
the two sections, than in the settlers of the different
States of both sections, and yet, no one will pretend
that want of homogenity in the settlers of the different States of either section has created any cause of
conflict or disturbance. We believe that, in no instance, can any essential difference between the people of the two sections be traced to want of homogenity in the original colonists.

The effect of climatic causes upon individual character is plainly seen in the change produced in representative men even, who have removed from the
one section into the other. They have invariably,
within a short time, not only conformed to the customs and institutions of the people of their adopted
section, but have partaken of all their peculiarities
and prejudices.

The continuance and growth of the system of
slavery have also been determined principally by the
influence of climate. When England first conceived
the policy of introducing African slaves to this country, and during the period of their early importation,
there existed no greater prejudice against the system
at the North than at the South. The same cause
induced the largest importation into the South, and
subsequently the abandonment of the system at the
North, and its growth at the South. It is plain that
climate has substantially controlled the fortunes of
this institution in this country from the commence-

ment.  Slave labor was not, and could not be
made profitable under the cold climate of the North;
hence it was discontinued.  In the Border or intermediate states, the system, as would be expected if
climate controls its destiny, has been continued with
a feeble growth; and, beyond them, under the well-
defined climate of the South, the slave population
has largely increased, and now constitutes the principal laboring class of that section.

But it is claimed, although the circumstances and
continued existence of the institution of slavery may
have been determined by the influences of climate,
yet that the institution itself has been influential in
creating a landed aristocracy at the South, which
has possessed itself largely of the social and political
powers of that section.  It has, undoubtedly, like
every other institution at the South, exerted an influence in the formation of its social and political
systems.  The influences of climate, and of the conditions it has been instrumental in creating, necessarily act and react upon each other, and all contribute more or less in the formation of the peculiar
systems which exist at the South.  Yet slavery has
not been a primary cause, nor has it had a controlling influence on either the social or political condition of the Southern people.

It will be difficult to prove that the institution of
slavery has given rise to any of the prominent social
or political phenomena that have been manifested at

the South. Its influence has been to increase and
intensify, rather than to originate, social and political idiosyncracies. We believe that, if slave labor
had never been employed at the South, there would
have grown up in that section a landed aristocracy,
which would have wielded a large share of social and
political power.

There is an inevitable tendency to inequality of
wealth in all warm countries, especially during the
early periods of their development. It is shown in
the possession of large landed estates by the few,
while the great masses of the population are mere
laborers, with neither the incentives nor means of
acquiring capital enjoyed by the laborers of more
temperate regions. There is nothing in the circumstances or history of the South to exempt its people
from the operations of this general law established
by climate. Inequality in wealth is inevitably followed by inequality in social and political power.
Without slave labor, the great landed proprietors of
the South would have constituted an aristocracy,
with powers differing only in degree from those exercised by the same class in the past; and if the institution of slavery shall be abolished, yet the negro
will remain. and in time it will be proved how much,
if at all, his social and political power will be increased, and consequently the power of the aristocracy diminished, by the change.

If these views are correct, then all of the impor-

tant differences between the people of the South and
of the other sections arise from, or their conditions
are determined by, the influences of climate.   If the
climate and soil of the North were similar to the
climate and soil of the South, the people of the
North to-day would be employed in the cultivation
of cotton, rice, and sugar-cane, to which commercial
and manufacturing interests would be subordinate;
and in sentiments, customs, and institutions, we
should be assimilated to the people of the South.
Under these conditions, even the institution of
slavery would afford no cause of difference or
offence between the sections, as there is every reason to believe it would be approved and sustained
alike by the people of both.

   If the above views are correct, it is evident, also,
that the influential differences between the two people cannot be removed by any human agency.   The
material interests of the South may be prostrated
for the time, but they cannot be made to conform to
those of the other sections.   The laws which govern
labor at the South may be suspended through violence, yet it will be impossible to substitute for them
the laws which control the labor of the North.   The
moment that force is withdrawn, the people of the
South will engage in the same pursuits as in the
past, and the character and conditions of its labor
will be determined by influences over which enactments of Congress can have but little control.   Nei-

ther will it be possible, by force or statute, to change the great characteristics of the people of the South. The causes which have produced them cannot be destroyed. Their operations may be disturbed by the violence of civil war, but when the struggle is over, and peace resumes its sway, they will again exert their silent influences, as in the past, upon the characters of those who shall people the States of the South. It is impossible to efface the marked differences in the characters of the two people by the exertion of any force. No policy which the general Government can adopt, can produce homogenity between the inhabitants of the two sections. There is no power in legislation that can compel the inhabit· ants of South Carolina and Georgia, or even of Illinois and California, to conform their institutions, habits, and modes of thought to those which govern the people of New England. Nor would the attempt to reduce the character of the people of the entire country to a single type be materially aided by a thorough change of population at the South. If the white race of that section should be completely exterminated, and its place filled by a people representing the most extreme Northern sentiments, we believe that within the time of one generation there would be developed quite as much difference in interests and character between the people of the two sections as has ever existed in the past; and that if the new population should prove to be more ener·

getic and more jealous of its rights than that which preceded it, there would exist greater cause of apprehension of hostilities between the two people, with no additional protection to sections under the Constitution, than has ever existed in the past. The abolition of slavery would remove the moral elements which have contributed so much to fire the heart of the North in the present struggle, without essentially modifying any of the prominent causes of dispute between the two sections.

But it may be asked how has it happened that, with such radical differences between the people of the two sections, both have lived together in peace under one flag for nearly eighty years, and enjoyed under it, during that period, unexampled prosperity. The answer to this is, that these results have been achieved through the beneficent operations of our peculiar system of government. The peculiarity of the system is in the divisions of power between the local or State governments and the General Government. The basis of the system is local self-government; its fundamental principle is, that the people of each considerable geographical section have the exclusive power of legislation and control, in all matters which pertain to their peculiar interests, customs, and institutions. Upon this basis is built the general or federative government, for the management of the external relations of the several States, and for their general protection. The Gen-

eral Government was framed by the Governments of
the different States through a Convention, and con-
sented to by their peoples. Their object in establishing it was to give additional security, strength,
and vitality to the local or State governments. As
Governments generally, are established for the purpose of affording protection to the individuals of the
community in the enjoyment of their natural rights
and of organizing and directing their aggregate force
against enemies from abroad, so the General Government was established, for the purpose of affording
protection to individual States in the enjoyment and
exercise of their rights under the system of local
self-government which had grown up, and for the
purpose of organizing and directing their aggregate
strength against foreign aggressors.

It is to this system that the people of the country
are indebted for their success in the past. Under
it, each State managed its own affairs, and exercised
exclusive control in all matters which pertained to
the domestic happiness of its people. We believe
that this system is the only one that could have secured the political co-operation of the people of the
two sections in the past; that a consolidated government would have signally failed of this object;
and that even a despotic government would have
been unable, by the exercise of any force, to have
compelled a political unity of the two people for
eighty years.

The dissatisfaction which culminated in the present struggle, arose, not from any dislike of our system of government, but from a jealousy lest the powers of the General Government should be perverted to the subversion of the principles of local self-government. The cause of the dissatisfaction was stated by President Lincoln in his inaugural message, March fourth, 1861, in the following language: "Apprehension seems to exist among the people of the Southern States, that by the accession of a Republican administration, their property, their peace, and their personal security are to be endangered!"

This apprehension existed, and was wide-spread, and whether justified by facts or not, induced the people of the Southern States to make an attempt at separation from the control of the General Government. If the facts justified the apprehension, they would also justify the people of the South in their revolutionary attempt. Under a General Government like ours, if a majority of the people and States unite for the determined purpose of oppressing the minority, or of interfering with its constitutional rights, the minority will have just cause for apprehension. For under the forms of law, through a gradual perversion of the spirit and intent of the Constitution, and by an exercise of questionable powers against which there may be no means of immediate redress, much injustice may be done to the rights and interests of the minority. The justification of a resort to revolutionary measures, which such acts by the majority would afford, is plainly stated in the message of President Lincoln above quoted from. He says: "If, by mere force of num. bers, a majority should deprive a minority of any clearly written constitutional right, it might in a moral point of view, justify revolution—it certainly would, if such right were a vital one." It is true, further, that if a majority shall have combined for the declared purpose of depriving the minority of any clearly written Constitutional rights, the minority is not bound to wait till the blow is struck, till its liberties are within the grasp of a hostile power, but is justified in adopting measures to avert the threatened calamity; and, unfortunately perhaps for the peace of Nations, the people whose rights are endangered are, in each case, the sole judges of the exigency, and necessarily make the decision under circumstances of passion and excitement. President Lincoln, in the same message, challenged reference to a single instance in which a plainly written provision of the Constitution had ever been denied, and disclaimed, for himself and his party, any intention of interfering with the constitutional rights of the people of the Southern States. We believe it true that a large majority of the party which elevated him and his administration to power, had not, at the time, an intention of violating clearly written constitutional rights: yet, the circumstances connected with the organization of the party, its history, the subjects on which it based its political platform, and the declarations of many of its representative men, of its intentions, were such as would naturally tend to excite jealousy in the minds of the people of the Southern States, and such as called, on the accession of that party to power, for an explicit and emphatic declaration of intentions from its representatives in Congress, which they persistently refused to make. The result was, the civil war which has now been waged upon a gigantic scale for four years.

All the important questions which now agitate the public mind, arise out of the state of affairs which this struggle has developed. By far the most important of these arise out of the issues presented, which affect the future existence of our system of government.

The liberties, happiness, and prosperity of the people of the country, in the future, depend upon a correct decision of these questions. Towns that have been destroyed may be rebuilt; interests that languish may be revived; wealth that has been sacrificed may be replaced, through the energy and enterprise of the people; and immigration may, in part at least, supply to the industry of the country a population in the place of that the war has destroyed. But the liberties of the people once stricken down—the American system once abandoned to despotic rule—if not lost for ever, can be rescued only after long years of suffering, through the terrible and desperate struggles of an oppressed people.

Our experience as a people since the adoption of the Constitution, has demonstrated the wisdom of our political system, and confirmed the faith of its founders that it was adapted to the exigencies of the country through all coming time. The dangers that have threatened, and troubles that have visited the country, have been caused by real or apprehended perversions of the system; and our experience, especially during the last four years, has demonstrated the necessity of additional securities for the future maintenance of the system. All our difficulties have resulted from the development of the different interests of the respective sections, to which there was given no adequate defensive powers in the organism of the General Government. The danger to the system from this source did not escape the attention of the framers of the Constitution. After determining upon the powers to be delegated to the General Government, and consequently the powers to be reserved to the States and the people, their attention was directed to the subject of the interests of minorities which might be endangered by the action of the majority, in the administration of the affairs of the General Government. They believed it to be unsafe to intrust power in the hands of the majority, with no other restrictions than mere constitutional prohibitions would afford. They recognized the truth, that

the great governing principle of majorities, as of individuals, is self-interest, and that the former are
more unscrupulous in the exercise of power for the
advancement of their interests, than the latter; and
they feared that, under a General Government, framed
upon a democratic basis and invested with the powers of the purse and the sword, the majority could
and would adopt measures with but little regard to
their effect upon the interests of the minority; and
saw that the only way to prevent such abuse was to
give to the minority a power in the government itself, to prevent the adoption of unfriendly measures.
Consequently, they sought to ascertain what classes
of States or individuals might be endangered through
the exercise of the powers of the General Government, with a view to give them a defensive power.

The small States were regarded as in a position
of danger, as it was evident that a few of the large
States, having a community of interests and a majority of the voters of the country, might unite, and
obtain control of the several departments of government. After full discussion, the dangers from this
source were provided against, by giving to each
State an equal representation in one branch of the
Government—the Senate; thereby conferring upon
the small States equal powers with the large ones,
in preventing the enactment of laws which they
might deem unfriendly to their interests.   No injurious effects in the legislation of the country have

resulted from this anti-democratic feature in the Government, and it has served to prevent not only conflicts, but even jealousies, between these two classes of States.

Pending the discussion in the Convention, upon the subject of the large and small States, Mr. Madison said: "He admitted that every peculiar interest, whether in any class of citizens or any description of States, ought to be secured as far as possible." That "whenever there is danger of attack, there ought to be given a constitutional power of defence." But he contended that the great difference of interests did not lie between the large and small States, but, 'That it lies between the Northern and Southern, and if any defensive power were necessary, it ought to be unitedly given to these two interests." Mr. Pinckney said there was " a real distinction between the Northern and Southern interests;" and that: "These different interests would be a source of oppressive regulations, if no check to a bare majority should be provided." Mr. King said: "He was fully convinced that the question concerning a difference of interests did not lie, where it had hitherto been discussed, between the great and small States; but between the Southern and Eastern." He said: "He was not averse to giving them (the Southern) a still greater security, but did not see how it could be done." Colonel Mason said: "If the Government is to be lasting, it must be founded in the confidence and affections of the people, and must be so constructed as to obtain these. The *majority* will be governed by their interests. The Southern States are the minority in both Houses. Is it to be expected that they will deliver themselves bound hand and foot to the Eastern States; and enable them to exclaim, in the words of Cromwell upon a certain occasion: "The Lord hath delivered them into our hands ?"

Notwithstanding the members of the Convention saw plainly the necessity of giving a defensive power to sections in the Constitution, yet, unfortunately for the peace of the country, they adopted no provision for the purpose. It is evident from the published debates, that such a defensive power was not provided, from an apprehension that the additional inequalities of powers in the departments of the government, which a provision adequate for this purpose would constitute, might peril the ratification of the system by the people. If such a power had been given in the Constitution, the controversies and jealousies that have arisen between the sections in the past, would have been avoided: and there would have been no occasion for the discussion of the question of the right of secession, which is practically only a question of the right of peaceable revolution.

But our experience in the past is chiefly valuable for the light it throws upon the path of our duty in the future. Whether, under the circumstances of the people of tho two sections at the time of the adoption of tho Constitution, a defensive power to sections was necessary or not, it is evident that, with the great subsequent increase of population, and vast development of resources, not only in the Northern and Southern, but in the other great divisions of the country, such a power is now indispensable, not only to secure the future co-operation of the people of the South, but to preserve the union between the people of the East, West, and Pacific Coast.

We believe that, if a defensive power to the different sections shall be given in the government itself, all controversies and jealousies in the future will be prevented, and that, with this security, the Southern States will be induced voluntarily to resume their places in the Union; and the people of the whole country, sadder but wiser from the experience they have suffered, will heartily cooperate for the accomplishment of the great mission which we still hope God has designed for the people of this continent. With nothing to excite ill-feeling, the people of each section will continue to develop their peculiar form of civilization under the beneficent and harmonizing influences of free institutions; and all jealousies against the General Government being removed, there will spring up in the hearts of the people a spirit of national unity, which will be confirmed and strengthened with the growth of the population and development of the resources of the country.

But it may be contended that, if the concurrence of the people of all the sections is required in the enactment of laws, the Government will be necessarily weak.    On the contrary, such a requirement would give to it additional strength.    It would bring to the support of its measures the people representing every interest of the country, instead of, as now, those representing only the majority interests. When we refer to the strength of a government, we should remember there are two classes of governments; the one depending for its strength upon its independence of the consent of the governed, and the other depending for its strength upon the voluntary consent of the governed.    Our government is of the latter class.    Its strength depends upon the approval of its measures by the people, and the larger the numbers that approve its acts—especially if they represent the different interests of the country —the greater the strength of the government.    The truth of this is verified by many instances in our experience.    The disaffections in New-England, which deprived the country of the cordial support of her people in the war of 1812, and the disturbance in South-Carolina in 1830, resulted from the exercise of powers by the General Government without the concurrence of the people of all the sections.

The grant of such a defensive power to sections would undoubtedly tend to modify the legislation of the General Government.    It would restrict action upon subjects affecting the different interests of the sections, and prevent the passage of acts for the promotion of the interests of the majority, to the prejudice of those of the minority, except with the consent of the latter. Upon referring to the powers delegated to the General Government by the Constitution, it will be seen that there are but few subjects within their legitimate reach upon which there would exist a difference of opinion between the people of the several sections; and that, even if legislation upon those subjects which affect the different interests of sections should be confined to the adoption of such measures only as would promote equally the interests of all, no interest would seriously suffer. But it would not be thus confined. Each section having peculiar interests, mutual concessions would be made, and the legislation would conform to the highest interests of the whole people.

The importance of giving such a defensive power to sections cannot be overestimated. Without it, the American system cannot be sustained in the future. It is not to be disguised that there are many influential men in power, and connected with it, who are enemies of the American system, and determined upon its overthrow. They would build upon its ruins a new and, as they assert, a stronger government, based upon powers independent of the consent of the governed. Some boldly proclaim their purpose; others, knowing the strength of the attach-

ment of the people to the principles of the system
they would subvert, seek to promote their object
through a system of covert and indirect attacks·
Appreciating the defenceless position of the system,
and believing that it can only be preserved through
the adoption of additional securities, they protest
strongly against all compromises and guarantees, and
point to our difficulties in the past, which were occasioned by a deficiency of guarantees. as proof that
the principles of the system are inadequate for the
exigencies of the country.

It is also strongly asserted by the enemies of the
system, that additional defensive powers to sections
are called for, only to satisfy imperious demands of
the people of the South.   This is untrue.   Although
indispensable to secure their voluntary co-operation,
they are not less important for the protection of the
rights and interests of the people of the other sections, in the future.

Upon the sectional questions out of which our
present difficulties sprung, the people of the West
acted with the people of the East.   But if the
Union shall be restored, without the adoption of additional guarantees for sections, new jealousies and
questions of conflict of interests will arise, upon
which the people of the East cannot expect the co-
operation of the people of the West.   Heretofore
the political action of the West has been largely influenced by the dependence of its interests upon the

capital of the East; but when, with the development of its resources, it is relieved of this dependence, its people will be governed in their political
action by the controlling interests of their section.
The great interest of the West, as of the South, is
agriculture; and this will inevitably insure political
co-operation between the people of these sections
upon all important questions that may arise in the
future, from conflicts of interests. It is plain that
the people of the Eastern States cannot, in the future, exert the control they have in the past, over
the people of other sections; and that, within a
brief period, the various agricultural interests of the
country will be able to control the legislation of the
General Government. When that time shall come,
the people of the Eastern States will fully appreciate the importance of defensive powers to sections,
in the organism of the Government.

We can have no doubt of the ultimate triumph of
the American system over its enemies, if the educated conservative men of the country shall prove
faithful in the performance of their duties. The
friends of the system are not confined to the conservative party of the country. Many influential
members and presses of the Administration party
are among its zealous defenders, and there are plain
indications that they are not blind to the dangers to
which the system is exposed. But, more important
than these, history proves how difficult it is for the

executives of government to effect a permanent change in the institutions of a country, even amid the distractions of civil war.

Although there have been not infrequent instances, in the history of civilized nations, of patient submission to usurpations and gross perversions of the powers of government during the pendency of a great struggle, yet, in nearly every instance, when the crisis had passed, the people have demanded and obtained, often after a protracted struggle, a return to the principles and system of government with which all their habits of thought and recollections of the past were indentified.

We believe this struggle will tend to confirm the attachment of the people to the principles of the American system. They have been educated under, and all their recollections of the past are connected with, the most beneficent system of government the world has ever known. For nearly eighty years, we and our fathers enjoyed the most ample protection ever afforded by any system of government, without the imposition of a burden that could be felt. The evils that have befallen the country have not resulted from any defect in the principles of the system, but from the insufficiency of the provisions for the prevention of jealousies and conflicts between the people representing the different great interests of the country. And when the passions and excitements of the struggle are over, we believe the people will return to the system with a love stronger than in the past; and, profiting by the terrible experience' through which they shall have passed, will, without the change of a single principle, adopt additional guarantees, which will insure to each great interest and section such ample protection tha there will be no opportunity, even for jealousy, in the future.

# CAUSES OF SECTIONAL DISCONTENT.*

There are no facts in the experience of a Government more deserving of thorough investigation by the student of political history, than those which relate to periods of popular discontents, from which no government of any considerable antiquity has ever enjoyed immunity.

It is from the study of the history of such periods that we learn the defects of the system of government, or discover the impolicy with which it has been administered. Although in times of peace and quiet the causes which produce discontent may be actively at work, yet they are often so remote as to escape the attention of contemporaneous statesmen; or, if detected and explained, their operations are so intermingled with the general and prosperous current of public affairs, that it is difficult to persuade those who administer the Government of their importance, or of the dangers with which they are fraught.

*Published in the Southern Review, July, 1868.

But when popular discontents come, and events happen which interfere with the harmonious co-operation of the Government and the people, the existence and operations of influential disturbing causes are no longer doubtful, and an investigation of their origin and progress is demanded by the exigencies which are created.

But, important as is an accurate knowledge of the causes of an existing discontent by the Government, that it may devise a permanent remedy, yet experience has shown that this knowledge is rarely attained during the continuance of the discontent. Indeed it is doubtful if any instance can be adduced from history, of a discontent culminating in actual conflict, which the Government at the time attributed to the real causes. The explanation of this is to be sought in the fallibility of those who administer the Government, and in the complicated circumstances connected with the origin and development of the causes themselves.

In a large majority of instances, the formidable discontents which have arisen in civilized communities have had their origin in systematic oppression of the people by the Government, or in the destruction of those securities against future oppression which the people have acquired, often through desperate struggles, and for the preservation of which they are animated with the greatest jealousy and zeal. Although in the progress of discontents other causes have frequently supervened, and sometimes partizan or moral and religious forces have been brought into requisition, yet they have served in each instance only to accelerate and give intensity to, rather than retard the progress of, the great primary causes.

In the instances of discontent which have resulted from measures of Government either indiscriminately oppressive of all the great interests of the people or subversive of their securities, the connection between cause and effect would seem to be too plain to admit of any doubt. Yet in these instances, when the measures of the Government have not been adopted for the tyrannical and wicked purpose of oppressing the people, those in authority have rarely comprehended, and more seldom acknowledged at the time, the real origin of the dissatisfaction. In the adoption of the obnoxious measures they have been governed by erroneous views of their relations to the people, and have proceeded upon the assumption, that their paramount duty was to maintain and strengthen the prerogatives of government, and that the interests of the people should always be subordinate to any policy which they might deem expedient for this purpose. Their plea has invariably been the exigencies of the State. They have consequently treated as groundless all complaints of the people which have followed upon the adoption of their measures, and attributed their inevitable discontents to the prevalence of a spirit of insubordination and sedition. It has been only when the discontents have become so formidable as to cause serious alarm, that they have been led to an impartial consideration of the real causes, which they have often comprehended and acknowledged too late to prevent the overthrow of the government.

In the more frequent instances of discontent which have resulted from measures of government oppressive of a portion only of the great interests of the people, or endangering their securities, the investigation of the causes is often, at the time, a more difficult and complicated task. The oppressive measures may have been adopted by those who administered the Government, from the best of motives, and with a sincere desire to subserve the highest interests of the people. Their authors may have been insensibly under the undue influence of the important interests which their measures tended to promote to the prejudice of the rest, and have deemed the policy they have adopted necessary for their successful operation, without sufficiently weighing the effect upon other interests; or they may have acted without a knowledge of the requirements of such other interests, especially when those interests have been local and remote from the seat of Government, or not ably represented in its administration.

The complaints of the people representing such oppressed interests have been addressed not only to the administrators of Government, but to the people representing the favored interests. whose opinions would be naturally and strongly in support of the measures complained of, and who have invariably co-operated with the Government to sustain and vindicate its policy upon the most plausible pretexts. The Government in these instances has had the numerical and moral strength of a large party of the people deeply interested in the support of its measures.    Partisan and local feelings have been strongly enlisted in their favor and added intensity to the discontent, which, when not allayed by a repeal of the obnoxious measures, has invariably resulted in most bitter and sanguinary conflicts.

That measures of government thus generally constitute the primary cause of popular discontents, not only experience, but a knowledge of the nature of mankind furnishes abundant proof.   It is difficult to conceive of a discontent pervading large and intelligent classes of people, or entire communities. and resulting in forcible resistance to the authorities, which did not have its origin in the conduct of the Government.   The people, unless actuated by the belief that systematic measures of Government are unjust and oppressive of their interests, or subversive of their just securities, can have no adequate motive for making the vast sacrifices, and incurring the tremendous responsibilities, which a resistance to the Government necessarily involves. Every interest of the people is on the side of peace and tranquillity. When the conduct of the Government is substantially just, the tendency in the people is to an affection for it. They have lived under and enjoyed its protection, and have learned to conform their opinions, habits. and modes of thought to its requirements. Even when the form of the Government is arbitrary, the people become accustomed to its rule. and endure occasional oppression not only without complaint, but without destroying their feelings of attachment to it. In the words of the American Declaration of Independence "All experience hath shown that mankind are more disposed to suffer while evils are sufferable than to right themselves by abolishing the forms to which they are accustomed."

But, while it is true that the primary causes of great popular discontents are to be sought in oppressive or dangerous measures of Government, yet experience has proved that in the progress of the discontents, the people often act without reasonable prudence or discretion. It rarely happens that they are wise in their modes of seeking redress, or judicious in the extent of their demands. They feel that their important interests are disregarded, or their securities imperilled, often without comprehending fully the most expedient remedy. The strongest passions are aroused. The people are inflamed by mutual contact, and not infrequently act with reckless impetuosity, and rush madly into the greatest dangers, from which they cannot reasonably hope for a successful issue.

It is our purpose in this article to make an inquiry into the primary causes of the three great discontents which have existed in this Country since the adoption of the Federal Constitution;—the discontent of New England in the war of 1812; the discontent of South Carolina in 1832; and the discontent which pervaded the Southern States in 1860; and to show the modes of redress, and the nature of the interposition proposed or adopted, in each instance, by the disaffected, against the authorities of the United States.

In this inquiry we propose to confine ourselves principally to the evidence furnished in each instance by the authoritative statements and declarations of the disaffected. This is proposed, not that it is the only evidence upon the subject, or that it is conclusive; but because it is evidence which is important and in its nature unmistakable, and because it has not generally received that consideration to which we believe it is entitled in discussions of the causes of discontents. The evidence is important. For if grievances exist, those who suffer, or deem their important interests endangered by them, are best capable of judging of their nature, and have the strongest motives for tracing their antecedents. Be-

sides, history teaches that the causes to which discontented communities have at the time attributed
their dissatisfactions, have been generally determined by the calm and dispassionate judgment of
posterity to be the correct ones. The importance
of this evidence in our own experience will be more
manifest, if it shall appear upon investigation, as we
think it will, that in the several discontents to which
we have referred, occurring at different periods, pervading the people of different sections, and arising
under different circumstances, the discontented in
each instance attributed their grievances to the same
general primary causes; and if it shall also appear
that the causes stated have been adequate to produce the results, and that, under our system of Government as organized by the Constitution, there has
been opportunity for their operations.

The primary causes of all our discontents, according to the concurrent testimony of the disaffected
at the different periods, are to be sought in attempts,
or apprehended attempts, by the majority of the
aggregate people of the country representing the
great interests of a section, or by a combination of
the people representing the great interests of different sections, to subordinate to their requirements,
through measures of the General Government, the
people representing the interests of the weaker sections. It requires no argument to prove that, in a
country with such a variety of great interests, geo-

graphically separated, as exist in the United States, the danger of such attempts is always imminent, unless such effectual checks are provided in the organism of the Government itself, as to preclude the reasonable probability of their being successful.

In the Constitution careful provisions were made with a view to prevent the exercise of such power. The authority of the Federal Government which it created, was expressly limited, its power distributed among different·departments, and in one branch of the Legislative Department, the Senate, an equal representation was given to all the States; so that no law could be enacted without the concurrence of a majority of the States.   In addition to the security to minority interests, which these protective provisions in the organism of the Government would give, it was believed that the fact that the several communities of each great section were to retain their political organizations, through which they could easily combine to resist encroachments upon their rights, or the rights and liberties of their people, would tend strongly to discourage partial legislation by the Federal Government.

These securities were provided in accordance with the requirements which it was supposed the circumstances of the country at the time demanded.   The only sections then peopled were the Eastern and Southern, and between the interests of these sections, the Constitution established a balance of power which it was deemed would afford to each ample protection.

But such was the wonderful development of the country, that within twenty-five years after the adoption of the Constitution, five new States were admitted into the Union, one by the separation of Vermont from New York, and *four* from the recently settled territories of the West and South-West. The admission of these States, and their consequent representation in the Federal Government, materially changed the balance of power of the different interests, as the interests of a majority of the States and people admitted were largely indentified with the interests of the South.

With their admission sprung up jealousies in the Eastern section, as the Southern and South Western States had the power to control the legislation of the Federal Government.

Opportunities for the exhibition of this feeling of jealousy were afforded in the circumstances and policies which preceded, and culminated in, the war with England in 1812. The predominant interest of the Eastern States at that time was commerce, and that of the Southern and South Western States agriculture. The Embargo act, which went into operation in 1808, and the Non-intercourse Act passed in 1809 in retaliation for the restriction imposed upon our commerce by France, in the adoption of the Berlin and Milan decrees, and by Great Britain in the adoption of the British Orders in Council, operated most injuriously upon our commerce; and the commercial States looked forward to a war with England, which it was believed must result, as ruinous to the interests and destructive of the prosperity of their section. So strong was the feeling excited against the restrictive policy of the Federal Government, that, although the war with England which followed was declared for the purpose of preventing foreign interference with our commerce, and for the protection of our seamen, yet it early met with a spirit of the most determined opposition from the commercial States.

The feeling of opposition to the war in the commercial States increased with the progress of the struggle, and the adoption of the measures which were deemed by the Federal Government necessary for its successful prosecution. In October, 1814, in response to memorials from a large number of towns, a resolution was reported in the House of Representatives of Massachusetts, "That twelve persons be appointed as delegates from this Commonwealth to meet and confer with delegates from the other New England States, or any other, upon the subject of their public grievances and concerns," &c., which was adopted by a vote of 260 to 90. The Senate concurred in the resolution, and on the 18th of October both Houses in convention elected the delegates by a vote of 226 to 67. The Legislature directed that copies of their proceedings be transmitted to the authorities of the several States. The Legislatures of Connecticut and Rhode Island were then in session and immediately passed resolutions in favor of such a convention, and elected delegates. The Legislature of Connecticut designated the 15th day of December following for its convocation. The Legislatures of New Hampshire and Vermont were not in session, but delegates were appointed from one or more counties of each. The convention assembled at the time designated, and continued in secret session· for three weeks. The result of its deliberations was embodied in a report which was signed by all the members, copies of which were directed to be transmitted to the Governors of the several New England States.

This report is of great importance as the authoritative statement of the people of New England upon the subject of the alleged grievances which had produced the wide-spread discontent which then prevailed. The convention was composed of delegates elected by the Legislatures of three of the New England States, and by conventions of the people in the other two. The members of the convention were the ablest representative men of New England. The report, with a copy of the proceedings of the convention, excepting the debates, is published in the volume of Mr. Dwight, who was secretary of the convention.

Upon the question of the primary causes of the
discontent, the report says, "Events may prove that
the causes of our calamities are deep and permanent.
They may be found to proceed, not merely from the
blindness of prejudice, pride of opinion, violence of
party spirit, or the confusion of the times; but they
may be traced to implacable combinations of individuals, or of States, to monopolize power and office, and to trample without remorse upon the rights
and interests of commercial sections of the Union.
Whenever it shall appear that these causes are radical and permanent, a separation by equitable arrangement will be preferable to an alliance by con-
straint, among nominal friends, but real enemies,
inflamed by mutual hatred and jealousy, and invi-
ting, by intestine divisions, contempt and aggressions
from abroad." Referring to the past policy of the
Government, the report says, "The administration,
after a long perseverance in plans to baffle every effort of commercial enterprise, had fatally succeeded
in their attempts at the epoch of the war.   Commerce, the vital spring of New England's prosperity,
was annihilated.   Embargoes, restrictions, and the
rapacity of revenue officers, had completed its destruction.   The various objects for the employment
of productive labor, in the branches of business dependent on commerce, have disappeared.   The fish-
eries have shared its fate.   Manufactures, which
government has professed an intention to favor and

to cherish, as an indemnity for the failure of these branches of business, are doomed to struggle in their infancy with taxes and obstructions, which cannot fail most seriously to affect their growth." Of the danger to which the commercial States, being in the minority, were subject to, the report says, "Whatever theories upon the subject of commerce have hitherto divided the opinions of statesmen, experience has at last shown that it is a vital interest in the United States, and that its success is essential to the encouragement of agriculture and manufactures, and to the wealth, finances, defence, and liberty of the nation. Its welfare can never interfere with the other great interests of the State, but must promote and uphold them. Still, those who are immediately concerned in the prosecution of commerce will of necessity be always a minority of the nation. They are, however, best qualified to manage and direct its course by the advantages of experience, and the sense of interest. But they are entirely unable to protect themselves against the sudden and injudicious decisions of bare majorities, and the mistaken or oppressive projects of those who are not actively concerned in its pursuits. Of consequence, this interest is always exposed to be harassed, interrupted and entirely destroyed upon pretence of securing other interests." And further, "No union can be durably cemented, in which every great interest does not find itself reasonably secured against the encroachments and combinations of other interests."

The convention adopted resolutions recommend-
ing the Legislatures of the several States represented to authorize immediate and earnest application to be made to the Government of the United
States, requesting its consent to some arrangement
whereby these States might assume the defence of
their territory, and be allowed a portion of their
taxes for the expense of the same; and recommen-
ding that the Governors of each of these States be
authorized by their Legislatures to raise and equip
men for the purpose of repelling any invasion of
their territory, which should be made or attempted
by the public enemy.   It also proposed amendments
to the Constitution of the United States to the following effect : 1st. That Representatives and direct
taxes should be apportioned among the several
States according to their respective numbers of free
persons.   2nd. That no new State be admitted without the concurrence of two-thirds of both houses.
3rd. That Congress should not have power to lay
any embargo on vessels for more than sixty days.
4th. That Congress should not have power to inter-
dict commercial intercourse with other countries,
without the concurrence of two-thirds of both houses.
5th. That Congress should not make or declare any
war with a foreign power, without the concurrence
of two-thirds of both houses.   6th. That no person
thereafter naturalized, should hold any civil office

under the authority of the United States. And 7th. That the same person should not be elected President of the United States a second time, nor a President be elected from the same State twice in succession.

Upon the proposed amendment relating to the admission of new States, the report says, "This amendment is deemed to be highly important, and in fact indispensable. In proposing it, it is not intended to recognize the right of Congress to admit new States without the original limits of the United States, nor is any idea entertained of disturbing the tranquillity of any State already admitted into the Union. The object is merely to restrain the constitutional power of Congress in admitting new States. At the adoption of the Constitution, a certain balance of power among the original parties was considered to exist, and there was at that time, and yet is among those parties, a strong affinity between their great and general interests. By the admission of these States that balance has been materially affected, and unless the practice be modified must ultimately be destroyed. The Southern States will first avail themselves of their new confederates to govern the East, and finally the Western States, multiplied in numbers, and augmented in population, will control the interests of the whole. Thus for the sake of present power, the Southern States will be common sufferers with the East, in the loss of permanent anvantages. None of the old States can find an interest in creating prematurely an overwhelming Western influence, which may hereafter discern (as it has heretofore) benefits to be derived to them by wars and commercial restrictions."

The foregoing extracts show plainly the causes to which the convention attributed the discontent of the people of New England, and the permanent remedies they deemed essential for their future protection.

The convention also suggested immediate remedies in the event that its complaints should be unheeded by the Federal Government, which it claimed might be legitimately resorted to. A recurrence to them is important both to show the spirit that actuated the members of the convention and to explain the views of the people of New England at that early period upon the rights of the States.

The report of the convention states, "That acts of Congress in violation of the constitution are absolutely void, is an undeniable position. It does not, however, consist with the respect and forbearance due from a confederate State towards the General Government, to fly to open resistance upon every infraction of the Constitution. The mode and the energy of the opposition should always conform to the nature of the violation, the intention of its authors, the extent of the injury inflicted, the determination manifested to persist in it, and the danger of delay. But in cases of deliberate, dangerous, and palpable infractions of the Constitution, affecting the sovereignty of a State, and liberties of the people, it is not only the right but the duty of such a State to interpose its authority for their protection, in the manner best calculated to secure that end. When emergencies occur which are either beyond the reach of the judicial tribunals, or too pressing to admit of the delay incident to their forms, States which have no common umpire must be their own judges, and execute their own decisions. It will thus be proper for the several States to await the ultimate disposal of the obnoxious measures recommended by the Secretary of War, or pending before Congress ; and so to use their power according to the character these measures shall finally assume, as effectually to protect their own sovereignty, and the rights and liberties of their citizens.' It further claimed in reference to the rights of the respective governments that, 'it is as much the duty of the State authorities to watch over the rights *reserved*, as of the United States to exercise the powers which are *delegated*.' The convention further resolved that if the application to the Government of the United States should be unsuccessful, if peace should not be concluded and the defence of these States should continue to be neglected, then it would, in the opinion of the convention, 'be expedient for the legislatures of the several States to appoint delegates

222 OF SECTIONAL DISCONTENT.

to another convention, to meet at Boston, in the State of Massachusetts, on the third Thursday of June next, with such powers and instructions as the exigency of a crisis so momentous may require.'

The convention adjourned without day, January 5th, 1815. A few days after its adjournment, the treaty of peace with Great Britain, which had been signed while the convention was in session, reached this country and was immediately ratified by Congress. Thus happily the immediate cause of dissatisfaction was removed and the discontent allayed.

The passions of the people, which had been intensely excited during the war, soon subsided with its termination. In the general rejoicing upon the return of peace, partisan and sectional animosities were for the time forgotton. James Monroe was elected President in 1816, having received the unanimous vote of every electoral college but three, and re-elected in 1820, having received every electorial vote but one. The epoch of his administration has been often referred to as the era of good feeling. Yet during this period, causes were at work which were destined to result in discontent of a most formidable character. The exigencies created by the war afforded the opportunity for their developments.

A large public debt had been contracted, for the payment of which it was necessary that extraordinary provisions should be made. In 1816 the

Tariff was revised, and the duties on imposts largely increased. The revision was made particularly
with a view to revenue, but it necessarily operated
to give incidently increased protection to domestic
manufactures. Encouraged by this act, and by the
favorable circumstances of the country, manufactures
were rapidly developed, and before the close of
President Monroe's administration, constituted an
important and influential interest in large sections
of the country. With their growth came demands
for still further protection, and in the Congress of
1823 and 1824 a revision of the tariff of 1816 was
proposed with a view to discrimination for the purpose of protection. This proposition was warmly
discussed. The friends of the American system, as
the advocates of a tariff for the purpose of protection styled themselves, claimed that additional protection was needed, temporarily, at least, not only to
secure the introduction of new branches of manufactures, but to sustain those already established. They
claimed further, that although manufactures especially benefitted the sections of the country in which
they were established, yet that their successful operation inured to the advantage of the whole country,
by increasing its aggregate wealth and resources,
and by relieving it, in the event of a war, of all dependence upon the manufactures of other countries.

The enemies of a protective tariff opposed the revision on the ground that the Constitution granted

no express power to the Federal Government to lay imposts for the purpose of protection, and that no such power could be legitimately exercised as an incidental right. They admitted that, under the Constitution, Congress could lay imposts to defray the necessary expenses of the Government, which might incidentally operate to protect domestic manufactures ; yet that Congress had no authority to lay a tariff for the purpose of protection to which the raising of a revenue would be incidental and subordinate.

They also contended that the protection of the Government was not necessary to the healthful growth of manufactures, and that the principal effect of high protective duties was to stimulate manufactures unduly, and to enrich the large capitalists who control their operations.

They asserted further, that a tariff for protection was necessarily based upon discriminations injurious to the interests of the staple-growing States, and that it deprived the people of those States of the right they claimed, of selling in the highest market, and purchasing in the lowest.

Notwithstanding these objections, a revision of the tariff was made in 1824, by which largely increased protection was given to domestic manufactures. The act caused great dissatisfaction among the people of the Southern States. But it was acquiesced in, with the hope that the policy it embodied would be abandoned upon the extinction of the public debt, which it was believed would soon be accomplished.

In 1827 the subject was again agitated, and a bill was proposed in Congress for increased protection to woolens.  This attracted the attention of those engaged in other branches of manufactures, and was followed by a convention of the friends of a high protective tariff at Harrisburg, in July of the same year.  The manufacturers of cotton and woolen goods of the Eastern States, the iron manufacturers of Pennsylvania and the growers of wool and hemp of the Western States were fully represented in the convention.  It was difficult to harmonize the various conflicting interests represented; but, after much discussion, a system of increased duties was agreed upon, which secured the co-operation of all the large manufacturers.

In the next Congress the subject was again discussed, upon a bill proposing largely increased protective duties on all articles of manufacture ; which passed by a vote of 105 to 95 in the House of Representatives, and by a vote of 26 to 21 in the Senate and was approved May 19, 1828.  The passage of this act and the determination manifested by the majority to make the system of protection a permanent one, caused great excitement and intense dissatis-faction throughout the staple-growing States, which remonstrated through their Legislatures against the measure as unconstitutional and oppressive of their interests.

In his annual message to the Congress of 1831, President Jackson announced that the public debt would soon be entirely paid, and recommended the reduction of duties to the amount needed for the payment of the ordinary expenses of the Government. The recommendation was considered by Congress, which passed an act diminishing the duties on articles not affecting the interests of the manufacturers, without reducing the duties on manufactured goods. This act was approved July 14, 1832, and tended greatly to increase the excitement which prevailed in the Southern States, as it indicated a determination to persist in the protective policy, notwithstanding the payment of the public debt. Resistance to the enforcement of the act was openly advocated. The Legislature of South Carolina convened October 22d, and on October 26th passed an act by the necessary majority vote of two-thirds of the members, authorizing a convention of the people, to meet at Columbia, on the 19th day of November following, to determine the course to be pursued by the State in view of the dangerous condition of affairs which existed. Delegates were chosen, and the convention assembled at the time and place appointed. The subject for the consideration of which the convention was called, was referred to a committee, which, on the the 24th day of November, made a re-

port, setting forth the grievances of the people of
the State, and proposing an ordinance for adoption
by the convention, which was adopted by a vote of
136 ayes and 26 noes. The convention also adopted two addresses, one to the people of South Carolina and the other to the people of the other States
of the Union. These papers and the report subsequently made to the convention on 'The Force Bill,'
so-called, may be considered as authoritative statements of the people of South Carolina upon the subject of their alleged grievances.

Upon the question of the primary causes of the existing discontent, the report on the Force Bill, after
reciting the measures which had been adopted by the
Federal Government tending to the prostitution of
our system of Government to the arbitrary will of the
aggregate majority, which if persisted in would result in a consolidated Government, states, 'And what
is it to the Southern States to be subjected to a consolidated Government ? These States constitute a
minority and are likely to do so forever. They differ in institutions and modes of industry from the
States of the majority, and have different, and in some
degree, incompatible interests. It is to be governed, not with reference to their own interests, but according to the prejudices of their rulers, the majority. It has been truly said that the protecting system constitutes but small part of our controversy
with the Federal Government. Unless we can ob-

tain the recognition of some effectual constitutional check on the usurpation of power, which can only be derived from the sovereignty of the States, and their right to interpose for the preservation of their reserved powers, we shall experience oppression more cruel and revolting than this.'                    •

The immediate cause of the discontent is stated at length in the report first made to the convention, from which we give the following extract : 'The laws have accordingly been so framed as to give a direct pecuniary interest to a sectional majority, in maintaining a grand system by which taxes are in effect imposed upon the few, for the benefit of the many;—and imposed too, by a system of indirect taxation, so artfully contrived, as to escape the vigilance of the common eye, and masked under such ingenious devices as to make it extremely difficult to expose their true character. Thus under the pretext of imposing duties for the payment of the public debt, and providing for the common defence and general welfare (powers expressly conferred on the Federal Government by the constitution,) acts are passed containing provisions designed exclusively and avowedly for the purpose of securing to the American manufacturers a monopoly in our markets, to the great and manifest prejudice of those who furnish the agricultural productions which are exchanged in foreign markets for the very articles which it is the avowed object of these laws to exclude. It so happens, that six of the Southern States, whose industry is equal to only one-third part of the whole Union, actually produce for exportation near $40,000,000 annually, being about two-thirds of the whole domestic exports of the United States. As it their interest so it is unquestionably, their right, to carry these fruits of their own honest industry to the best market, without any molestation, hindrance, or restraint, whatsoever . and subject to no taxes or other charges, but such as may be necessary for the payment of the reasonable expenses of the Government. But how does this system operate upon our industry? While imposts to the amount of ten or twelve per cent., (if arranged on just and equal principles) must be admitted to be fully adequate to all the legitimate purposes of Government, duties are actually imposed (with a few inconsiderable exceptions) upon all the woolens, cottons, iron and manufactures of iron, sugar, and salt, and almost every article received in exchange for the cotton, rice, and tobacco of the South equal on average to about fifty per cent.; whereby (in addition to the injurious effects of this system in prohibiting some articles, and discouraging the introduction of others) a tax equal to one-half of the first cost is imposed upon cottons, woolens, and iron which are the fruits of Southern industry, in order to secure an advantage in the home market, to their rivals the American manufacturers of similar articles

equivalent to one-half of their value, thereby stimula-
ting the industry of the North and discouraging that
of the South, by granting bounties to the one and
imposing taxes upon the other.'

The immediate remedies proposed are set forth in
the ordinance which was adopted. It declares the
Tariff acts of 1828 and 1832 unconstitutional, and
null and void, and not binding upon the State, its
officers or its citizens; forbids any officer, State or
Federal, to enforce the revenue laws within the
limits of the State; and further declares, that, if any
attempts shall be made on the part of the Federal
Government to enforce said acts or to coerce the
State, the people thereof would forthwith proceed to
organize a separate Government.

In the address to the people of the other States of
the Union, the right of the State to nullify is claimed.
The report asserts 'That the States have the right in
the same sovereign capacity in which they adopted
the Federal Constitution, to pronounce, in the last
resort, authoritative judgment on the usurpations of
of the Federal Government, and to adopt such measures as they may deem neccessary and expedient to
arrest the operation of unconstitutional acts of that
Government within their respective limits.... And
the obligation of the oath which is imposed, under
the Constitution, on every functionary of the States,
to "preserve, protect, and defend" the Federal Constitution, as clearly comprehends the duty of protect-

ing and defending it against the usurpations of the Federal Government, as that of protecting and defending it against violation in any other form or from any other quarter......But clear and undoubted as we regard the right, and sacred as we regard the duty of the States to interpose their sovereign power for the purpose of protecting their citizens from the unconstitutional and oppressive acts of the Federal Government, yet we are as clearly of the opinion that nothing short of that high moral and political necessity which results from acts of usurpation, subversive of the rights and liberties of the people, should induce a member of this confederacy to resort to this interposition. Such, however, is the melancholy and painful necessity under which we have declared the acts of Congress, imposing protecting duties, null and void within the limits of South Carolina......There is no right which enters more essentially into a just conception of liberty, than that of the free and unrestricted use of the productions of that industry wherever they can be most advantageously exchanged, whether in foreign or domestic markets. South Carolina produces, almost exclusively, agricultural staples, which derive their principal value from the demand for them in foreign countries. Under these circumstances. her natural markets are abroad; and restrictive duties imposed upon her intercourse with those markets, diminish the exchangeable value of her productions very nearly to

the full extent of those duties.' In this address the
following proposition for adjustment was made:
'But we are willing to make a large offering to preserve the Union; and with a distinct declaration
that it is a concession on our part, we will consent
that the same rate of duty may be imposed upon the
protected articles that shall be imposed upon the un-
protected, provided that no more revenue be raised
than is necessary to meet the demands of the Government for constitutional purposes, and provided
also, that a duty, substantially uniform, be imposed upon all foreign imports.'

On the 10th day of December following, President
Jackson issued a proclamation asserting his right
and duty as President, to execute and enforce all
laws of the United States within the State of South
Carolina, and declaring that this duty would be faithfully performed. In it he admitted that the people
of that State had 'indeed felt the unequal operation
of laws' which might 'have been unwisely but not un-
constitutionally passed,' but that 'inequality must
necessarily be removed'; and made to them a patriotic appeal to refrain from the commission of acts
which might require the employment of force on the
part of the Federal Executive.

The apprehension of open collision between the
Federal authorities and the people of South Caroli-
na caused great excitement throughout the country.
The Legislature of Virginia, with a view to avert the

danger, on the 26th day of January, 1833, adopted resolutions requesting the authorities of the State of South Carolina to rescind the ordinance of nullifica- tion, or at least to suspend its operation until the close of the first session of the next Congress; and requesting of Congress that it would modify the Tariff acts to effect a gradual but speedy reduction of the revenues of the General Government to the standard of the necessary and proper expenditures for the support thereof. The resolutions also de- clared that the people of Virginia expected, and had a right to expect, that the General Government and the Government of South Carolina would carefully abstain from any and all acts calculated to disturb the tranquility of the country, or endanger the ex- istence of the Union.

The subject had been considered in Congress be- fore the date of the adoption of these resolutions, and a Bill had been proposed, known as the Com- promise Bill, providing for a gradual reduction of duties. Mr. Clay, the acknowleged leader of the par- ty in favor of the American System, advocated its passage in a statesmanlike and patriotic speech, from which we make the following extract : 'It has been intimated by the Senator from Massachusetts, that. if we legislate at this session on the tariff, we would seem to legislate under the influence of a panic. I believe, Mr. President, I am not more sensible to danger of any kind than my fellow-men are generally. It perhaps requires as much moral courage to legislate under the imputation of a panic, as to refrain from it lest such an imputation should be made. But he who regards the present question as being limited to South Carolina alone, takes a view of it too much contracted. There is a sympathy of feeling and interest throughout the whole South. Other Southern States may differ from that as to the remedy to be used, but all agree, (great as, in my humble judgment, is their error,) in the substantial justice of the cause. Can there be a doubt that those who think in common will sooner or later act in concert? Events are on the wing, and hastening this co-operation. Since the commencement of this session, the most powerful Southern member of the Union has taken a measure which cannot fail to lead to the most important consequences. She has deputed one of her most distinguished citizens to request a suspension of measures of resistance. No attentive observer can doubt that the suspension will be made. Well, sir, suppose it takes place, and Congress should fail at the next session to afford the redress which will be solicited, what course would every principle of honor, and every consideration of the interests of Virginia, as she understands them exact from her? Would she not make common, cause with South Carolina, and if she did, would not the entire South eventually become parties to the contest? The rest of the Union might put down the South, and reduce it to submission; but to say nothing of the uncertainty and hazards of all war, is that a desirable state of things? Ought it not to be avoided if it can be honorably prevented? I am not of those who think that we must rely exclusively upon moral power, and never resort to physical force. I know too well the frailties and follies of man, in his collective as well as individual character, to reject in all possible cases, the employment of force; but I do think that when resorted to, especially among the members of a confederacy, it should manifestly appear to be the only remaining appeal.'

The Compromise Bill was passed March 2d, and on March 15th the Convention of South Carolina, by a nearly unanimous vote, rescinded its ordinance of nullification.

The relief of the discontent in South Carolina and the other staple growing States, through the adoption of a magnanimous and conciliatory policy on the part of the Federal Government, gave much ground for the hope that even if the guaranties of the Constitution should prove inadequate for the security of minority interests, yet that the wisdom, patriotism, and spirit of devotion to the Union in the American people, would in the future prevent a reference to the last resort on issues involving material interests alone. But other and powerful causes were already actively at work, and their influence had been felt before the time of the adoption of the Compromise measures on the tariff.

The American system of negro slavery which prevailed in all the States at the time of the adoption of the Federal Constitution, having proved unprofitable under the climate of the Eastern and North-Western States of the Union, had been gradually discontinued in those States; and at the time of the disaffection in South Carolina, had been abolished by law in all excepting the Southern States.

Soon after the adoption of the Constitution, movements were inaugurated by citizens of States in which the system had been discontinued, for the purpose of procuring legislation by the Federal Congress on the subject of slavery. These movements were supported by only an inconsiderable number of individuals, and for many years attracted but little public attention. But the application of Missouri for admission into the Union in 1818, opened a wide field for agitation upon the subject. A bill was reported in the House of Representatives, by the Committee to which the subject was referred, for the admission of Missouri as a State into the Union upon an equal footing with the original States. An amendment was proposed to the bill in the House prohibiting slavery in the State. This was agreed to by the House, but nonconcurred in by the Senate. Neither branch would recede, so the bill was lost.

The application was renewed at the next session.

After a protracted discussion in the House of Representatives, which called forth much sectional feeling,
a motion was made to amend the bill reported for
its admission, by adding to it a new section prohibiting slavery forever in all territories ceded to the
United States by France, under the name of Louisiana, not included within the limits of Missouri, north
of a proposed conventional geographical line.

The adoption of this amendment was strenuously
opposed by the Southern members.  They contended
that Congress had no constitutional power to deprive settlers of the the common territory of the
Union of the privilege of taking with them and employing their slaves, which they owned as property
by the laws of the States from which they emigrated;
and further, that the passage of the act would establish a most dangerous precedent, as it would initiate a policy of arbitrary discriminations by the Federal Government upon the subject of slavery in the
territories.  But the amendment was adopted, and
the bill as amended, passed both Houses and was
approved by the President.

Thomas Jefferson, then in the retirement of private life, had watched the progress of the discussion
with intense interest, and immediately upon the passage of the act wrote to a friend:  'But this momentous question (the Missouri one) like a fire-bell in
the night, awakened me and filled me with terror.
I considered it at once as the death-knell of the

Union.    It is hushed indeed for the moment; but, this is a reprieve only, not a final sentence.    A geographical line, coinciding with a marked principle, moral and political, once conceived and held up to the angry passions of men, will never be obliterated; and every new agitation will mark it deeper and deeper.' This great and sagacious statesman was not mistaken.    Although hushed for the time, the agitation upon the subject was renewed a few years later with increased warmth.

In 1830, societies were formed in the Northern States for the avowed object of abolishing slavery in the States, or dissolving the Union.    Contributions were made, zealous agents employed, and the Southern mails flooded with documents of a most incendiary character, which excited a feeling of indignation mingled with alarm throughout the South. These societies rapidly increased and the numbers of their members were augmented.    Public attention in the Southern States was called to their movements. The people of Charleston, South Carolina, held a large public meeting, May, 11, 1835, for the purpose of preventing 'seditious pamphlets from being sent through the mail.'    Resolutions were adopted and a large number of copies of the proceedings of the meeting were published and sent to different parts of the country.

Public meetings in reference to it were held in Boston and other cities of the North. The meeting in Boston was held, May 21st, in Faneuil Hall. It was a very large and respectable meeting, and was addressed by Harrison Gray Otis, Richard Fletcher, Peleg Sprague, and others. Judge Sprague in his speech upon the occasion, referred to the dangerous character of the movement in the following prophetic language: 'If these abolitionists shall go on, if their associations shall continue to increase, if their doctrines shall spread and their measures be adopted until they become the general sentiment and action of a majority of the people of the North, and this shall be known, as known it will be, at the South, the fate of our government is sealed—the day that sees such a consummation, will look only upon the broken fragments of our Union.'

The meeting adopted a series of resolutions in which they declared, 'We solemnly protest against the principles and conduct of the few, who in their zeal would scatter fire-brands, arrows, and death.'

But the spirit of abolitionism was not to be thus silenced. New conflicts of material interests were continually springing up between the sections; and political leaders soon learned the power of this new agency in uniting and intensifying the feelings of the people in support of their political measures. For a few years there was no open co-operation between the abolitionists and politicians, as no important issues could be framed on the subject of slavery which could be defended on constitutional grounds.

But the proposition to admit Texas as a State into the Union in 1844, and subsequently the establishment of Governments for the territories acquired in the war with Mexico, afforded an opportunity which was not neglected, for the organization of a political party upon important anti-slavery issues which were claimed to be within the purview of the Constitution.

This party asserted that Congress has a right to prohibit the people of the Southern States from emigrating with their slaves into any portion of the public domain, and claimed that by the act of 1820 the country was committed to the policy of slavery-exclusion in the territories. The immediate, avowed object of this party was to prevent, through legislation of the Federal Government, the admission of any new State into the Union with a Constitution legalizing slavery, and consequently to increase the number and preponderance of the free States in the Union.

The professed objects were purely moral ones, yet the dividing line between the slave and free States coinciding geographically with the line of demarcation between the conflicting interests of the country, a co-operation of material and moral forces was rendered inevitable on all great questions involving the material interests of the country.

The result which neither the conflict of interests nor the power of abolitionism had been able alone to accomplish, was destined to be consummated through the vigorous co-operation of both. With the power to subordinate the interests of the weaker section to those of the stronger, within the reach of the majority in the stronger section, and with great moral issues on which to inflame the people and vindicate their acts, a way was opened to political demagogues at the North for the establishment of a great sectional party with power to control the administration of the Federal Government.

The organization of this new party was the signal for fierce and desperate political conflicts. Based upon the great predominant interests of the majority section of the country, appealing to and reviving all the sectional prejudices of the past, and animated by the intolerant spirit of a bitter fanaticism, the political anti-slavery party of the North rapidly increased in numbers and power. It soon obtained the supremacy in the Governments of many of the free States, and in each instance of success pursued a most relentless and proscriptive course against the local minorities which attempted to arrest its progress. The administration of the Federal Government was looked upon as a barrier in the way of its success, and the authorities of the States in which it had control were invoked against the acts of the Federal Congress.

The legislature of Massachusetts, as early as the period of the admission of Texas, '*Resolved*, That Massachusetts hereby refuses to acknowledge the act of the Government of the United States authorizing the admission of Texas, as a legal act in any way binding her from using her uttermost exertions, in co-operation with her sister States, by every lawful and constitutional measure, to annul its condition and defeat its accomplishment.' A few years later the Legislature of the same State passed an act known as the personal liberty bill, intended to nullify within the Commonwealth the provisions of the act of Congress passed for the rendition of fugitives from service and labor; and as late as in 1856, '*Resolved*, That the Legislature of Massachusetts is imperatively called upon by the plainest dictates of duty, from a decent regard to the rights of her citizens and a respect for her character as a sovereign State to demand of the National Congress a prompt and strict investigation into the recent assault upon Senator Sumner, and the expulsion, by the House, of Mr. Brooks of South Carolina, and every other member concerned with him in said assault.'

Massachusetts not only claimed authority as a sovereign State, but the right to interpose that authority against acts of the Federal Government, which her Legislature and not the Judicial Tribunals of the country might deem to be unconstitutional. The Legislatures of other States of the North asserted the same authority and passed personal liberty bills similar to that enacted by the Legislature of Massachusetts.

But the great immediate object of the party was
to increase the relative power of the North, and
through a union of its people to obtain control of all
the Legislative Departments of the Federal Government. The numerical superiority of the people of
the North over the people of the South was so large
as to insure the election by it of the President and a
majority of the United States House of Representatives, upon any considerable unanimity of political
action. The Senate, representing the States, was
more equally divided; and although in this branch of
the Government, during the entire period of the
struggle, the North had a majority, yet it was so
small as not to be relied upon except on a thorough
union of the people of all the States. Thus the
struggle for slavery-exclusion in the territories became one of the deepest significance. Each party
contributed to the contest its most strenuous efforts.
For years this struggle for power in the Senate ab-
sorbed every other issue. The North, having the
control of two branches of the Federal Government
within its power, strove with the fiercest energy to
secure to itself the same predominance in the other
branch, that it might control the legislation of the
Federal Government. This accomplished, the Supreme Court of the United States would remain the
only obstacle to the complete perversion of all powers of the Federal Government to the arbitrary will
of a sectional majority. Systematic efforts were

made to destroy its influence. Its decisions were treated with contempt, and the tribunal itself traduced in political speeches and platforms. The people of the South, on the other hand, were united with the intensest zeal to retain their relative strength in the Senate of the United States. They felt that their negative power in this branch of the Government constituted the only barrier against oppression that remained; as under a sectional administration of the Government, decisions of the Supreme Court would be evaded or disregarded, and that eventually, by new appointments, the character of the tribunal would be radically changed. The prejudices as well as the interests of the respective sections were enlisted in the struggle.

At the North, the grossest misrepresentations were made by the political leaders to arouse and inflame the passions and jealousies of the masses. They declaimed to the people with effect, that in this contest for power, which it really was, the people of the South were striving for supremacy in the Federal Government; although the relative numbers of the populations of the respective sections were such as to render it impossible for the South in a sectional conflict, to control the election of President or of a majority of the House of Representatives, both of which would be necessary for such a consummation; and they attempted to justify their own sectional policies under most specious and fallacious pretexts.

A thorough amalgamation of political and moral issues was accomplished. The party of politics and conscience rapidly increased. It received a check from the compromise measures of 1850, but rallied to secure the supremacy of the North in the territory of Kansas, in anticipation of the application to it of the principles of the Legislation of 1850. But the Kansas issues proved insufficient. In 1858, a bold advance step was taken. The doctrine of the irrepressible conflict, substantially the doctrine of the early abolitionists, 'scattering fire-brands, arrows, and death,' was proclaimed by Messrs. Seward and Lincoln, and adopted by the party of which they were the acknowleged leaders. From this time Constitutional limitations and guarantees were disregarded, and an open appeal was made for a union of the people of the North against the people and institutions of the South. The appeal was successfully made, and in 1860 a President was elected on a platform based upon absolute slavery-exclusion in the territories, and a practical nullification of the decisions of the Federal Courts.

Deep-felt alarm pervaded the people of the Southern States. In December following the election, a convention of the people of South Carolina was held, and passed an ordinance of secession and adopted a declaration of the causes which it claimed justified the measure. We give the following extract from it :—

'We affirm that those ends for which this Government was instituted have been defeated, and the Government itself has been made destructive of them by the action of the non-slaveholding States.   Those States have assumed the right of deciding upon the propriety of our domestic institutions, and have denied the rights of property established in fifteen of the States, and recognized by the Constitution; they have denounced as sinful the institution of slavery; they have permitted the open establishment among them of societies whose avowed object is to disturb the peace and to endanger the property of the citizens of other States.   They have encouraged and assisted thousands of our slaves to leave their homes, and those who remain have been incited by emissaries, books and pictures, to servile insurrection.

'For seventy-five years this agitation has been steadily increasing, until it has now secured to its aid the power of the common Government.   Observing the forms of the Constitution, a sectional party has found within that article establishing the Executive Department, the means of subverting the Constitution itself.   A geographical line has been drawn across the Union, and all the States north of that line have united in the election of a man to the high office of President of the United States, whose opinions and purposes are hostile to slavery.   He is to be entrusted with the administration of the common Government, because he has declared that that "Government cannot endure permanently half-slave, half-free," and that the public mind must rest in the belief that slavery is in the course of ultimate extinction.

'This sectional combination for the subversion of the Constitution has been aided in some of the States by elevating to citizenship persons, who, by the supreme law of the land, are incapable of becoming citizens, and their votes have been used to inaugurate a new policy hostile to the South, and destructive of its peace and safety.

'On the 4th of March next this party will take possession of the Government. It has announced that the South shall be excluded from the common territory; that the judicial tribunals shall be made sectional, and that a war must be waged against slavery until it shall cease throughout the United States.

'The guarantees of the Constitution will then no longer exist; the equal rights of the States will be lost. The slaveholding States will no longer have the power of self-government or self-production, and the Federal Government will have become their enemies.

'Sectional interest and animosity will deepen the irritation, and all hope of remedy is rendered vain by the fact that public opinion at the North has invested a great political error with the sanctions of a more erroneous religious belief.

'We, therefore, the people of South Carolina, by our delegation in Convention assembled, appealing to the Supreme Judge of the world for the rectitude of our intentions, have solemnly declared that the Union heretofore existing between this State and the other States of North America is dissolved, and that the State of South Carolina has resumed her position among the nations of the world, as a free, sovereign, and independent State, with full power to levy war, conclude peace, contract alliances, establish commerce, and to do all other acts and things which independent States may of right do.

'And, for the support of this declaration, with firm reliance on the protection of Divine Providence, we mutually pledge to each other our lives, our fortunes and our sacred honor.'

The States of Georgia, Mississippi, Florida, Louisiana and Alabama, in January followed the example of South Carolina. On February 4th, a convention of deputies of the seceded States met at Montgomery, Alabama, to organize a Southern Confederacy, and on February 8th, adopted a Constitution for a Provisional Government. The Congress of the United States was at the time in session. Senator Crittenden, of Kentucky, the last of the great statesmen of his generation, proposed in the Senate, December 19th, a series of resolutions for adoption, with a view to relieve the apprehensions of the people of the South, and allay the existing discontent.

Intense excitement prevailed throughout the country. It was evident that unless Congress should take some decided action to relieve the discontent, seperation or war was inevitable. It was generally believed that nothing short of the adoption of the resolutions of Mr. Crittenden could effect the desired result. The resolutions were temperate. They were not intended to extend the rights of the people of either section under the Constitution; but to dispose of disputed questions by compromise, to reaffirm plain constitutional rights which had been threatened, and to afford to them additional protection. They were in accordance with the genius of our institutions, and were such as could have been adopted consistently with the honor of the country. The Southern members of Congress, including Mr. Jefferson Davis and Mr. Toombs, declared their willingness to accept of the resolutions as a final settlement of the difficulties, if adopted with the concurrence of the representatives of the dominant party; and expressed their opinion, that if thus adopted, the excitement at the South could be allayed.

The Legislative assemblies of Kentucky and Virginia adopted the resolutions. Conservative citizens in all parts of the country joined in earnest memorials to Congress, urging their adoption by that body. Mr. Pugh, Senator from Ohio, declared in his place in the Senate, March 3, 1861, that the resolutions 'had been petitioned for by a larger num-

ber of electors of the United States than any proposition that was ever before Congress.' But the resolutions met the united opposition of the representatives of the Republican party in Congress. They
were not adopted. The excitement at the South increased. Other States passed secession ordinances.
A war of sections followed. The North prevailed in
the conflict of arms. The great result upon the interests of the country, and the Union of the States as
organized by the Constitution, is to be determined
in the uncertain future.

# CLOSING ARGUMENT FOR PLAINTIFF,

IN CASE OF

GEO. W. STONE *VS*. WM. SEGUR *ET ALS*.

*in the Supreme Court, at Salem, Mass., November Term,*
1865. *Justice Gray, presiding.*

———

I have listened with attention to the eloquent remarks of the counsel who has closed in behalf of the
defendants, and am happy that I am able to agree
with him on many of the legal propositions he has
enunciated; but I regretted to hear from his lips, as
I know you gentleman of the jury did, expressions of
opinion that there is a spirit higher, nobler, and
rather to be emulated, than the spirit of what he was
pleased to style the cold law; and, to repeat the language of the counsel, that there is nothing to be ad-
mired in the spirit which a rigid adherence to rules
calls forth. I was pained gentlemen, to hear such
language from one sworn to fidelity to the law,
uttered in the very temple of justice itself, and in
the presence of so many of his fellow citizens.
But, perhaps, something should be pardoned
to counsel placed in the embarrassing position
of the counsel for the defendants, called upon to de-

fend plain and confessed violators of the law, and I trust that many of the expressions to which we have been obliged to listen were uttered without due consideration, under the pressure and excitement of the occasion.

The counsel for the defendants has attempted covertly, yet unmistakably, in his eulogistic language upon the spirit of license, to justify the outrages committed by his clients. In no part of his argument did he dispute the truth of the charges preferred against the defendants, or the illegality of their acts, and yet he found little if anything, to condemn, in all that was done. It will, I trust, require no argument from me to convince you, gentlemen of the jury, that the doctrine he addressed to you is entirely subversive of all law, and destructive of the peace and even the existence of civilized society. No one can be safe, gentlemen, if irresponsible men may at their pleasure take the law into their own hands, and order can never be preserved in communities where such a practice is permitted.

I need only to refer to the injustice and cruelty which mark every such violation of the law. Mobs not only usurp the province of judges and juries, but that of the law making power itself, and set at defiance all the salutary safeguards of innocence which have been established and confirmed by the wisdom of ages. Upon the strength of rumors circulated against an individual, an impromptu crowd, wild with excitement, determine to inflict summary punishment on the assumed offender. There is no form of trial—instead of the calm intellect and dispassionate judgment which alone should pass upon the guilt or innocence of any human being, is the tumult and madness of passion, strengthened and intensified by the presence and contact of numbers. In the place of a trial with all the presumptions and securities which the wisdom of the law has established, and at which the accused is confronted by his accusers face to face, is a sudden and summary judgment, not on evidence, but on wild report, and all this in the absence of the accused. The judgment is pronounced before the victim is aware even of the charge, and the first intimation he has is the presence of the mob to carry into execution the sentence they have passed: There have been not infrequent instances in newly settled portions of the country of executions by an infuriate populace, of criminals seized from the hand of the officers, whose offences had been determined under the law, who had been legally tried, convicted, and sentenced. In every such instance the cruelty of the actors has been revolting to humanity, and inflicted an indelible stain upon the community in which the outrage was committed. How much more revolting the spectacle, and terrible the catastrophe, when a band of infuriated men have not only taken the execution of a sentence out of the hands of the constituted authorities, but have prefaced the act by a summary, exparte, and extra judicial trial and judgment.

The facts in the present case afford a marked illustration of the doctrine of the counsel for the defendants, not only in the results to the individual, but to the community. A rumor was started against the plaintiff—men congregated; without even an inquiry into the truth of the rumor they rushed to the building on which the plaintiff was at work; the first salutation was a demand in loud tones that he should come down and deliver himself up to the crowd. He refused to comply with it, when one of the leaders discharged at him a revolver loaded with powder and ball, and was only prevented from repeating the act by the interference of his associates. Stones and other missiles were then thrown. The plaintiff, alarmed, sought refuge within the building. The doors to the lower floor which were fastened were forced open, and the crowd rushed to the room on the second floor into which the plaintiff had retreated. He was immediately seized, and dragged with violence down the stairs, kicked by his assailants, and then placed in the centre of the crowd and led to an appointed rendezvous, and on the way was struck a dastardly blow in the face. When he arrived at the place of destination, a line was formed and a vote taken, not upon the question of the guilt or innocence of the plaintiff, but solely upon the mode of punishment. It was proposed that he be tarred and feathered—the vote was immediately taken and resulted in a unanimous affirmative. After this, and you will judge, gentlemen, whether it was not the first opportunity he had to open his lips, upon the claim of a bystander that he ought to be heard, a vote was formerly taken, in the words of Brackett, one of the defendants, to allow him to speak. No accusation was preferred against him. He could only conjecture his assumed offence from the remarks of the mob on the way. He was asked only what he had to say. He replied that he had not made the remarks he understood were attributed to him, and reiterated, as he said upon the stand, the denial that he had said anything wrong or offensive. But his words reached only the seething passions of the mob. He was instantly seized, his hat was pulled from his head, his frock and shirt torn from his person, and the tar and feathers, which had been previously procured, were applied to his head and body, by the crowd, amid shouts of fiendish joy. He was then marched to the Town Hall, in which the teachers of the county were assembled at their annual gathering. Their approach was heralded by Rev. Mr. Clark, a clergyman of the village, who was presiding over the convention, and, as he stated upon the stand, the convention was adjourned at his suggestion, that the members might proceed to the balcony to witness the spectacle, thereby countenancing and approving the acts of the mob. After a

brief detention at this place, he was marched down
the street a short distance, and then placed in a boat,
and dragged to the beach, the crowd most of the
time attended by Mr. Galeucia, a constable of the
town, one of the defendants, who, as he stated on
the stand, at no time uttered a word of rebuke or
disapprobation. Upon the way dirt was thrown
upon his person. Finally, wearied of their efforts,
after a detention of from two to three hours they
permitted the plaintiff to return to his home. This
gentlemen, was a practical and full illustration of the
spirit which is higher and nobler than that of the
law.

Gentlemen, a case has been referred to in the testimony, which occurred more than half a century
since in a neighboring town, which affords the strongest illustration of the injustice and cruelty of judging a man without the law. Upon the strength of a
wild rumor, Skipper Ireson was seized, tarred and
feathered, placed in a cart, drawn from Marblehead
to Salem, and through the principal streets of this
city, attended by an indignant crowd repeating the
lines composed on the occasion, and familiar to all.
The old man never recovered from the effects of
this humiliation. Yet now it is well understood that
the rumor, upon the strength of which these outrages
were committed, was false. Gentlemen, no instance
of the acts of a mob can be adduced where cruelty
and injustice have not been done to the victim and

public decency has not been thoroughly outraged.

But I trust, gentlemen, it is not necessary before a jury of Essex County, to occupy time in arguments against the evils of lawlessness and license, or to remind the members of this tribunal of their own obligations to the law. I believe that, in your deliberations, you will be governed solely by the instructions you will receive from the Judge who presides over these deliberations. Let none of us assume to a knowledge higher than that of the law of the land, or aspire to a wisdom that is greater than the wisdom of the law. There can never be any excuse or palliation for any violation of the salutary regulations that are made for the protection of all. The law makes ample provisions for the conviction and punishment of all offenders against its majesty, and in instances of gross violations of the proprieties of life, in language uttered, which are not within the purview of the Statutes, there is always a sufficient punishment to the offender in the scorn and contempt in which he is held by the community.

The great object of law, gentlemen, is the protection of the citizen in social life; it throws around every individual, high and low, rich and poor, those beneficent and tranquilizing securities which no other human instrumentality can give. Without these securities, there can be no safety or happiness in life —without them the father, as he leaves his dwelling to perform the duties of his avocation, must feel a constant solicitude for the safety of those he leaves behind; and the wife and those of tender age will live in perpetual apprehensions, not only for their own safety but for the safety of him who has gone forth from the sacred precincts of home. There can be, gentlemen, there is, no safety for any one, anywhere, except under the protecting ægis of the law. It is not enough that laws be enacted alone—they must be respected and reverenced by the people, or the best code is but a solemn mockery and farce. Liberty, gentlemen, is not license, it is the right to do those things which the law does not prohibit; and the measure of liberty is in the amount of the protection which is assured the individual in doing all those things which he has a right to do under the law. Liberty is maintained in its highest perfection when the system of laws, or restraints upon the the actions of the individuals of society, is most wisely adjusted, and the conduct of all the members of the society is made to fully conform to its regulations. If under such a system of laws, or any system of laws, one member of society can with impunity do what the law does not permit, there is no liberty for any one, as all the other members can exercise the same power with the same impunity. If one man may violate the law in what he considers a good cause to-day, his neighbor, on the strength of the precedent it will afford, may violate it with impunity in what the former may consider a bad cause to-morrow. If one having the power to-day, exercises it against his neighbor for expressions of opinion which he does not approve; to-morrow the case may be reversed, and his neighbor may have and exercise the same power against him for the utterance of opinions which the former does not approve.

There is no safety anywhere or to anybody, except in an exact obedience to the laws; and if a jury in a case like this, to which public attention has been strongly directed, should fail to carry out plain provisions of the law, it would afford a precedent most dangerous for the future, and cause a general and prevading sense of insecurity among the people.

The counsel for the defendants has spoken of the effect upon the community of a verdict against his clients—that it would cause sorrow to those he styles the loyal portion of the community. I deem it, gentlemen, my duty to say that, if the case is proved against the defendants, the highest and holiest interests of the whole community demand that you shall give a verdict against them. Not only the interests of the community, but justice to my client, and I believe mercy to the defendants, require at your hands a rigid adherence to the provisions and rules of the law. With the spirit manifested by the defendants in the commission of the outrage for which they are prosecuted, in their subsequent acts, in their appearance on the witness stand, I believe that if they shall go from this trial unpunished, it will only incite them to further acts of lawlessness and outrage, for which a more severe punishment than can be meted to them in this case, will be inflicted.

What then, gentlemen, is the charge against the defendants to which your attention is directed?

The plaintiff alleges that, on the morning of the fifteenth day of April last, whilst at work painting the outside of a house in the town of Swampscott, he was approached by the defendants and others, and finally seized and outraged in the manner I have already stated. The defendants, in their answers to the plaintiff's declaration, only formally deny the allegations, and call upon the plaintiff, as they properly may under the law, to prove his case. They do not attempt to set up any justification, as in law they well know there can be none for the acts if proved as alleged against them.

There are only two questions for you, gentlemen of the jury, to pass upon.

1st—Did the defendants or any of them commit the acts alleged against them?

2d—If they, or any of them, did commit the acts, what is a proper compensation to the plaintiff for the injuries inflicted?

In regard to all but one of the defendants there is, there can be, no dispute. The proof submitted by the plaintiff against them is amply sufficient, but that is not all. Each one of the defendants has been

placed by his counsel on the stand, and has admitted
in detail his complicity with the outrage. So in regard to them there can be no doubt or question.
Their acts are not only proved, but confessed in
open court. In regard to the other defendant,
Galeucia, the constable, the evidence is that he, at
different times, walked by the side of the crowd and
did nothing and said nothing against the commission
of the outrage of which he was a witness. When on
the stand, he admitted that he did not attempt to
interfere with the proceedings of the mob, but said
that he tried to keep himself clear of any responsibility. His associate officer, Mr. Porter, on the cross-
examination, said that Galeucia lent to the mob the
official sanction of his presence. The acts of this
officer, gentlemen, are to be carefully scrutinized by
you. It was his sworn duty as an officer of the law
to preserve the peace, and it was plainly his duty to
attempt, at least, to put a stop to the gross violations
of law of which he was a witness. Yet, by his presence during the commission of these acts, without a
word or act of disapproval, he lent to the offenders his
countenance and approval of their proceedings, and
is liable as principal equally with those who took a
more active part in what was done. From the evidence, I believe that no one engaged in the transaction was more culpable than Mr. Galeucia, and I
trust you, gentlemen, will not relieve him of the re
sponsibility which he thus voluntarily assumed.

Upon the question of the amount of damages, the counsel for the defendants has claimed that you could only find such a sum as will be a compensation to the plaintiff for the injury done him, and that you should give no exemplary or vindictive damages. I agree fully with the counsel in this. This is a suit to recover only compensation for the personal injuries suffered by the plaintiff; the punishment for the disturbance of the peace of the community, and as an example in the future, is to be inflicted by indictment, by fine and imprisonment, by the criminal courts, under the direction of officers of the Commonwealth. It is only compensation that is sought for here, compensation for the bodily injuries inflicted on the plaintiff, the bodily pains and the mental suffering he endured. In due time, and before the proper tribunal, the defendants will be punished for their violation of the public peace. But the counsel for the defendants, for the evident purpose of affecting the amount of your verdict, enlarged with much eloquence upon the fact that a portion of his clients, and those most active in the commission of the outrage upon the plaintiff, were returned soldiers, and had served their country in the army of the Potomac. I deem it my duty to defend the army against the aspersion that is thus attempted to be cast upon it. There is no one who entertains a higher respect for the noble profession of arms than I do, and no one who appreciates more fully the courage of those who have fought their country's battles. Entertaining these sentiments, I must protest against all attempts to place such persons as these defendants in the position of representative men of the army with which they have been connected. It is well known that, although a large majority of the men who composed our armies were young men of character who returned from the field ennobled and refined by the discipline of the camp, yet that there were others who were mustered into the service and remained a longer or a shorter time, who were bad men when they entered, and much worse when they left the field. The true soldiers have been engaged in fighting against mobs for the maintenance of Government and law, and no class of our citizens will feel greater indignation at violations of peace and order at home than these men. You, gentlemen of the jury, have listened to the evidence of the acts of these defendants, and what is of greater importance you have seen them and heard them all testify from the stand. You are fully able to judge to which class those of the defendants who have been connected with the army, belong. I could ask for nothing more severe for those military defendants, than that they should be tried by a jury of their comrades whom they have so disgraced by their acts. Such men as those of the defendants who have been in the army are to-day, and will be more in the future, a terror to the community, and the sooner and the more emphatically they are made to feel the power of the law they have violated, the better it will be for all.

The counsel, who opened the case for the defendants, expressed indignation at the term which my able associate applied to the defendants in his opening argument, and referred with a great deal of enthusiasm to his clients as citizens, soldiers, fishermen and tradesmen. It is impossible for me to say how such conduct as we have proved against the defendants effects their counsel, but for my part I can only say that my client, as he looked upon the infuriate mob that surrounded him, might well have imagined himself in a den of human hyenas. Such utter violations of sacred personal rights, and gross injustice and cruelty as were practiced are entirely unprecedented in the history of the country. For these acts, gentlemen, I can conceive of no excuse or palliation.

The counsel who closed for the defendants seemed to be imbued with the same defiant spirit which has characterized his clients from the date of the commission of the outrage to the present time; the same spirit that incited the proceedings of the defendants on the fifteenth of April, their subsequent cowardly acts in destroying in the night time the growing crops of the plaintiff, and their conduct around his dwelling even whilst this trial has been proceeding. The counsel in his argument, justified the defendants, he gloried in their acts, and evidently considered the whole transaction as a commendable illustration of the true spirit of what he calls liberty. He seems fired with the spirit of the heated partizan in England, who exclaimed, "I wish I were free." "And are you not free," replied a friend, "can you not do as you please?" "yes," he replied, but I cannot make you do as I please." Is this the liberty the counsel pants for? It is the kind of liberty he has so eloquently eulogized. In his wild enthusiasm he has even defied the law and you gentlemen of the jury. He said to you, gentlemen, in reference to his clients that verdicts and judgment, might be repeated in vain—that their spirits could not be repressed. It will be your duty, gentlemen, to test the irrepressible spirit of these men by one verdict, and we will wait and see the effect. I believe it will be salutary and repressive.

Upon the question of damages, it may be useful to carefully consider all the acts of the defendants at the time of the commission of the outrage to ascertain fully the spirit by which they were animated, The greatest outrage was committed on the plaintiff, yet these irrepressible men were possessed of a spirit of lawlessness, or as their counsel prefers to style it, of liberty, which was not confined to acts against the plaintiff. On the way to the rendezvous, which was the village Post Office, the mob met a Mr. Reynolds on his wagon. He was admonished to leave at once, or as Mr. Brackett said, to make himself scarce as Mr. Brackett stated, he had uttered expressions similar to those rumor had attributed to the plaintiff, but upon cross-examination, Mr. Brackett was compelled to admit that he had never uttered a word.

They next pass Mr. Hill, the milk-man, just as the courageous Mr. Blaney struck the plaintiff on the face. Mr. Hill exclaimed, "It is too bad" whereupon a portion of the mob turned upon and severely beat him, and compelled him to take refuge in the woods. A little further on they met Mr. Alexander Greenlaw returning in a wagon from the village to his home. He was stopped, accused of using language similar to that attributed to the plaintiff, and threatened with a similar treatment, and, later still in the proceedings, one of the leaders of the mob said to a citizen who was gazing on the spectacle from his carriage, "This is the way we are going to serve the whole of you." Thus was fully manifested the spirit of these irrepressible men.

The details of the outrages on the plaintiff have been recited. As they transpired they called forth feelings and expressions of sorrow and indignation from every impartial witness of their atrocity. Mr. Atkins, a near neighbor of the plaintiff, testified that he felt so badly when he witnessed the spectacle that he immediately went into his house. Mr. Hill could not refrain from expressing his indignation, when he saw the plaintiff struck in the face. Mr. Greene when the plaintiff was about to be tarred and feathered, although from his testimony on the stand it appeared he was either in sympathy with or in fear of the rioters, cried out, "For God's sake let the man speak," and Mr. Leavitt in reply to a remark of Segur, one of the defendants, exclaimed, "It is the worst sight I ever saw." Such were the feelings which the acts of these irrepressible men excited in the breasts of honest citizens at the time, and such to-day are the feelings of all good citizens of Swampscott, whose peace has been so violently outraged by the wicked conduct of a portion of her misguided people.

In regard to the rumors against the plaintiff, there is no evidence that he ever uttered a word offensive to the most patriotic ear. He never did utter any. If it had been competent, we could have fully proved that the rumor which was circulated, upon the strength of which the outrage was committed, was devoid o truth; and it will be borne in mind, no two of the defendants gave the same version of the rumor itself.

The amount of the damages it is for you, gentle-men, to determine. It is for you to say what is a proper compensation to the plaintiff for all the in-jury that has been proved. A worthy and peaceable citizen, one who has ever been strictly faithful to all his obligations to the community and the coun-try, has been seized and treated with an inhumanity paralleled only in savage life, and it is for you, gentle men, to fix the compensation for the outrage.

The people of Essex County have been long distinguished as a law abiding, law sustaining people, and it is your responsible duty to see to it, gentlemen, that this reputation suffers no detriment at your hands. It is for you, gentlemen of the jury, to render such a verdict as you can in the future look back upon with satisfaction, and one that will meet with the approval of all good men in the community.

The jury returned a verdict against all the defendants, assessing damages in the sum of $800

www.ingramcontent.com/pod-product-compliance
Lightning Source LLC
Chambersburg PA
CBHW030731280326
41926CB00086B/1103